FALCON GUIDE®

Best Easy Day Hikes Series

Best Easy Day Hikes Redwood National and State Parks

D0311246

FALCON®

GUILFORD, CONNECTICUT
HELENA, MONTANA

AN IMPRINT OF THE GLOBE PEQUOT PRESS

08-CGH-020

Contents

Introduction 1
Zero Impact 3
Ranking the Hikes 5

The Hikes

1. Myrtle Creek Trail 7
2. Hiouchi Trail 11
3. Crescent Beach Trail 15
4. Hobbs Wall Trail and Trestle Loop 19
5. Damnation Creek Trail 24
6. Coastal Trail: Yurok Loop to Hidden Beach 28
7. Point St. George Trail 32
8. Carruthers Cove Trail 36
9. Ten Taypo–Hope Creek Loop 40
10. James Irvine–Miner's Ridge Loop 44
11. Fern Canyon Loop 48
12. Trillium Falls Trail 52
13. Ladybird Johnson Grove Trail 56
14. Tall Trees Grove Trail 59
15. Dolason Prairie Trail 63
16. Skunk Cabbage Trail 67
17. Rim Trail Loop 71
18. Trinidad Head Loop 76
19. Arcata Community Forest Loop 80
20. Headwaters Forest Trail 85
21. Hookton Slough Trail 90
22. Bull Creek Flats Loop 94

About the Author 99

The Redwood Coast

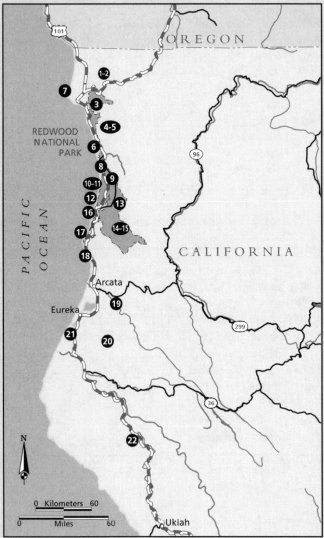

Introduction

Among out-of-staters, California is probably best known for its movie stars, wacky politics, and iconic landmarks like the HOLLYWOOD sign and the Golden Gate Bridge. With all the glitz and hype, it is easy to forget that California is also a natural wonderland, full of rich and varied landscapes. Nowhere is this more true than in the redwood parks of California's North Coast. Whether you like it wet, dry, high, low, perfectly level, or very nearly vertical, there is something here for you.

The obvious star of the redwood parks is *Sequoia sempervirens*, better known as the coast redwood—tallest living thing on Earth. Of the estimated two million acres of old-growth redwood existing at the time of European contact, only around 3 percent survive, most of them in the cluster of small parks that the hikes in this book explore. Sword ferns and cloverlike redwood sorrel carpet the forest floor under the thick, emerald canopies of these giants. In the east, the redwoods gradually give way to other species, including red and Douglas fir, Sitka spruce, incense cedar, Port Orford cedar, sugar pine, and several oak species. Directly on the coast, salt-sensitive redwoods leave a narrow strip to hardier plants such as Monterey cypress and coastal scrub species.

Wildlife here is easily as impressive as the flora. Hikers have a fair chance of seeing gray whales, sea lions, black bears, Roosevelt elk, and ospreys in appropriate spots and times. Mountain lions, bobcats, foxes, otters, marbled murrelets, and spotted owls also live here, though sightings are less likely. California's rivers host impressive seasonal salmon runs, although, like the redwoods, they're much diminished from historical levels.

Weather in the redwood region tends to produce wet winters and foggy summers, with summer heat increasing greatly just a few miles inland. Generally speaking, you are more likely to get rained on in winter, and seasonal bridges will all be removed at this time of year because creeks and rivers tend to swell dramatically with the rains. Since rain, wind, drizzle, and fog are common weather patterns on the coast in winter, you should bring waterproof shoes, wool socks, a good rain jacket, gloves, a hat, and even an extra set of dry clothes.

Rules and regulations vary from park to park and may change without notice. Check with the appropriate agencies before heading out, just to be sure. State parks generally require a day-use fee, but Redwood National Park and National Forest Service lands do not. Due to the ever-present fire danger, campfire permits are required on most public land throughout the state.

Zero Impact

The trails in the redwood parks of California's North Coast are quite popular and sometimes can take a beating. Because of their popularity, we, as trail users and advocates, must be especially vigilant to make sure our passing leaves no lasting mark.

These trails can accommodate plenty of human travel if everyone treats them with respect. Just a few thoughtless, badly mannered, or uninformed visitors can ruin the trails for everyone who follows. The book *Leave No Trace* is a valuable resource for learning more about these principles.

Three Falcon Zero-Impact Principles

- Leave with everything you brought.
- Leave no sign of your visit.
- Leave the landscape as you found it.

Most of us know better than to litter. It is unsightly, polluting, and potentially dangerous to wildlife. Be sure you leave nothing, regardless of how small it is. Pack out all of your trash, including such biodegradable items as orange peels, which might attract area critters. Also consider picking up any trash that others have left behind.

Follow the main trail. Avoid cutting switchbacks and walking on vegetation beside the trail. Select durable surfaces, such as rocks, logs, or sandy areas, for resting spots.

Don't collect souvenirs, such as rocks, shells, feathers, driftwood, or wildflowers. Removing these items will detract from the next hiker's experience.

Avoid making loud noises that may disturb others. Remember, sound travels easily along ridges and through canyons.

Finally, remember to abide by the golden rule of all hikers: If you pack it in, pack it out! Thousands of people coming behind you will be grateful for your courtesy.

Ranking the Hikes

Although the hikes in this book are relatively easy, some are longer and have more elevation change than others. Here's a list of the hikes in order of difficulty, from easiest to hardest.

21 Hookton Slough Trail

2 Hiouchi Trail

13 Ladybird Johnson Grove Trail

7 Point St. George Trail

1 Myrtle Creek Trail

11 Fern Canyon Loop

6 Coastal Trail: Yurok Loop to Hidden Beach

3 Crescent Beach Trail

17 Rim Trail Loop

8 Carruthers Cove Trail

18 Trinidad Head Loop

9 Ten Taypo–Hope Creek Loop

22 Bull Creek Flats Loop

12 Trillium Falls Trail

5 Damnation Creek Trail

10 James Irvine–Miner's Ridge Loop

19 Arcata Community Forest Loop

16 Skunk Cabbage Trail

14 Tall Trees Grove Trail

4 Hobbs Wall Trail and Trestle Loop

20 Headwaters Forest Trail

15 Dolason Prairie Trail

Map Legend

—=⟨26⟩=—	U.S. highway
—⟨1⟩—	State highway
▬▬▬	Paved road
▬▬▬	Featured gravel road
══════	Gravel road
▬▬▬▬	Featured unimproved road
=====	Unimproved road
▬▪▬▪▬	Featured trail
- - - - -	Other trail
✛	Airfield
⤫	Bridge
▲	Campground
∘	City
•—•	Gate
☆	Horse trail
🚶	Other trailhead
▢	Overlook/viewpoint
🅿	Parking
▲	Peak/elevation
🅰	Picnic area
■	Point of interest
—•—	Powerline
🚻	Restroom
≡	Steps/boardwalk
START 🚶	Trailhead
❺	Trail number
𝒊	Visitor information
∥	Waterfall
↯	Wetlands

1 Myrtle Creek Trail

Highlights: This is an easily accessible, short day hike with the feel of a backcountry wilderness area. The trail follows the course of a water diversion ditch that was used for a turn-of-the-twentieth-century hydraulic mining operation. Along the way, interpretive signs explain a little of the history and a lot about the diverse flora in the surrounding forest, part of the Myrtle Creek Botanical Area.

Distance: 2.1 miles out and back.

Approximate hiking time: 1.5 hours.

Best months: April through October.

Fees and permits: No fees or permits required.

Maps: USGS map: Hiouchi, CA; *DeLorme: Northern California Atlas & Gazetteer*: Page 22 B3.

Trail contact: Smith River National Recreation Area, Six Rivers National Forest, Gasquet; (707) 457–3131.

Finding the trailhead: From Crescent City, take U.S. Highway 101 north about 7 miles, then turn onto U.S. Highway 199 at the Grants Pass exit, heading northeast. Follow this 7 miles, past the Hiouchi Visitor Center (Redwood National Park). About a mile past the visitor center, pull off and park at the gravel turnout just south of the Myrtle Creek Bridge. The trailhead is just across the road, at a cut in the rocky bank.

The Hike

Crescent City investors had good reason to expect a return on their money when they founded the Myrtle Creek Mining Company in 1894. After all, placer mining (panning for gold) during previous years had turned up some impressive nuggets in the drainage. The largest single nugget found in

Myrtle Creek Trail

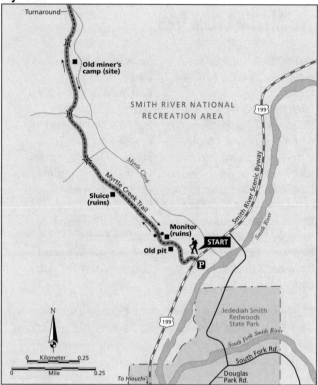

the creek was the size and shape of an ax bit and weighed in at a healthy forty-seven ounces. With the easy pickings gone, however, the new miners turned immediately to hydraulic mining, which allowed them to extract the tiny deposits left in the sand and soil. For a time the effort paid off, but by the early 1920s the gold had become too expensive to remove profitably, and the mine closed. Today only the ditch, a few pipes and trestle timbers, and the slowly healing scars remain.

The trail starts at a deep cut—a result of early hydraulic gold mining—in the steep uphill embankment lining US 199. The trail soon climbs up out of the cut and at 0.1 mile begins contouring around the slope through a lush second-growth mixed forest. Myrtle Creek is located in the transition zone between the coastal forest community, which includes redwoods, rhododendrons, and ferns, and the drier interior region dominated by knobcone pine. The watershed is made even more botanically diverse by the wet riparian habitat near the creekbed and the addition of rare serpentine soils. All these elements interact to create a very diverse range of conditions for plant life, which has lead to the Myrtle Creek area being designated one of six special botanical areas within Six Rivers National Forest. The trail has been outfitted with nature trail–style guideposts, and each of the fifteen interpretive stops has a small sign explaining a little about the cultural history or interesting flora to be found there. A brochure that goes into greater depth can be picked up at the information center in Hiouchi or at the National Forest office a few miles upriver in the town of Gasquet.

At the third stop on this self-guided tour, the trail begins to parallel a mining-era ditch that was used to channel water down to the big water cannons. The remainder of the hike follows this ditch, ending where the water was originally drawn from the creek, about a mile upstream.

From the turnaround point where the trail meets the creek, return the way you came to the trailhead.

Miles and Directions

0.0 Start at the little trail sign on the west side of the road. The trail heads steeply up through a cut in the bank.

0.1 A small fenced area to the left surrounds an old pit. From this point the trail follows the edge of a former mining sluice/ditch.

1.0 The trail crosses a plank bridge at a small waterfall. The creek is visible below to the right. About 50 feet later, the trail drops to creek level, revealing a nice soaking hole. This is the turnaround point. Return the way you came.

2.1 Arrive back at the trailhead.

2 Hiouchi Trail

Highlights: An easy hike through some top-notch old-growth redwood forest. As an added bonus, the hike follows the south bank of the jade-green Smith River, one of the largest undammed rivers left in the United States. In summer a seasonal bridge links up with the Jedediah Smith Redwoods State Park campground, but in winter you'll have it all to yourself.

Distance: 4.2 miles out and back.

Approximate hiking time: 2 hours.

Best months: April through October.

Fees and permits: No fees or permits required if accessed from the highway.

Maps: USGS map: Hiouchi, CA; *DeLorme: Northern California Atlas & Gazetteer*: Page 22 B3.

Trail contact: Jedediah Smith Redwoods State Park, Crescent City; (707) 464–3779; www.parks.ca.gov.

Finding the trailhead: From Crescent City, head east about 9 miles on U.S. Highway 199. A few miles before Hiouchi, and just before the Hiouchi Bridge (which crosses Smith River), pull off and park along the road. The trailhead is next to the highway sign beside the bridge.

The Hike

Jedediah Smith Redwoods State Park is named for a famous mountain man and explorer of the early nineteenth century. Smith was one of the first white men to visit extreme northern California. In 1827 the thirty-year-old Smith made his way up the Sacramento Valley, cutting west along the Trinity River to the Klamath River and downstream to the ocean. He then traveled north to Damnation Creek. Continuing north he eventually passed the mouth of the river that bears

Hiouchi Trail

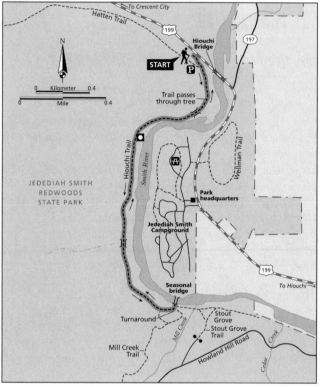

his name with a party of trappers in 1828. Jedediah Smith Redwoods State Park was created in 1929, a century after Smith's party passed by the area. The 10,000-acre park preserves some of the finest old-growth redwood groves in existence. The Hiouchi Trail explores some of these, and it also takes in some panoramic views of the wild and scenic Smith River along the way.

The hike begins at the south end of the Hiouchi Bridge, where US 199 crosses the Smith River on its way up to the Oregon border. The trail enters the forest at an unassuming little trail marker and parallels the south bank of the turquoise-colored Smith. The river's unique coloration can be traced back upstream to extensive deposits of serpentine, a rare gray-green mineral that forms the basis for soils in large swaths of the Six Rivers National Forest and Smith River National Recreation Area, which border the park.

The Smith River watershed is the largest completely undammed river system in California. Not surprisingly, it also has one of the healthiest fisheries of any river in the state—a fact not lost on anglers, who flock here to fish for salmon, steelhead, and cutthroat trout.

The bulk of the Hiouchi Trail follows the south bank of the Smith, where old-growth redwood specimens tower above the water right at the edge of the low bluffs. The trail builders seem to have had some fun in constructing the trail, running it up to the edge of the bluffs for several dramatic views, and even straight through a hollow redwood stump. The climax of the trail comes at the far end, when it reaches the park's crown jewel—Stout Grove. From here, a seasonal summer bridge heads across the river to the park campground. Return to the trailhead the way you came.

Miles and Directions

- **0.0** Start at the southwest end of the Hiouchi Bridge, on the east side of the highway. The trail follows the river east, then climbs a short series of steps and a couple switchbacks.
- **0.1** Hatten Trail merges into our trail from the right. Continue straight on the Hiouchi Trail.

0.3 The trail heads right through an old-growth redwood snag that has been hollowed out by fire.

2.1 End of the trail. To the left, a seasonal bridge crosses the river to the campground. The Mill Creek Trail is straight ahead; return the way you came.

4.2 Arrive back at the trailhead.

3 Crescent Beach Trail

Highlights: The trail crosses meadows and alder forests just inland from the broad, sandy shoreline of Crescent Beach. The easy grade and pastoral surroundings make for a very pleasant walk, which culminates with a short climb through denser coastal forest to the overlook above Enderts Beach. From here, hikers can enjoy an excellent view of the Pacific and the scenic shoreline stretching north to Crescent City.

Distance: 4.2 miles out and back.

Approximate hiking time: 2 to 3 hours.

Best months: April through October.

Fees and permits: No fees or permits required.

Maps: USGS map: Sister Rocks, CA; *DeLorme: Northern California Atlas & Gazetteer*: Page 22 C2.

Trail contact: Redwood National and State Parks, Crescent City; (707) 464-6101; www.nps.gov/redw.

Finding the trailhead: From Crescent City, take U.S. Highway 101 south 2 miles. Turn right (west) onto Enderts Beach Road. Follow this 0.4 mile, then turn left onto a long driveway leading up to a white house called Enderts Beach House (this is park property). Follow the road for 0.2 mile, parking in the small gravel lot behind the house. The trailhead is on the south side of the house, across from the garage.

The Hike

This trail could have easily been named the bridge trail, since it crosses what seems like a dozen small footbridges on its way down the coast. From the historic white ranch house at the trailhead, the path leads across the grassy meadows of former agricultural land—now making the slow transition back to

Crescent Beach Trail

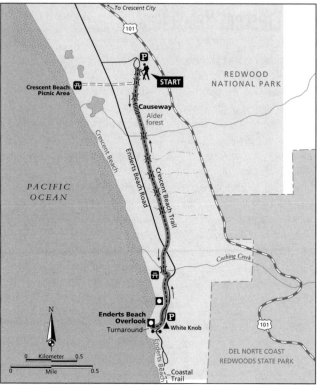

forest as brush and fast-growing alders gradually reclaim the fields. Aside from the many bridges, the trail consists mostly of mown grass. This makes for a nice, cushy walking surface, but it can also lead to a serious case of soggy feet, especially after rain or when morning dew is still fresh on the ground.

For most of its length, the trail keeps to the nearly flat strip of grassland and alder forest that's tucked neatly between the ocean and the coastal range to the east. This changes when the trail reaches Enderts Beach Road, a little more than a mile from the trailhead. Here the trail heads across the road and down to a little picnic area under a massive spruce tree. One last bridge awaits at the creek flowing through the hollow, then a final ascending leg as the trail climbs the coastal bluffs to the Enderts Beach Overlook and the turnaround point. In the decades before the National Park Service took over, the parking lot at the overlook served as the local Lover's Lane for Crescent City teenagers, who gave the spot the bawdy nickname "Endert's Knob."

From the overlook the view to the north is of the broad, curving beach that gives nearby Crescent City its name. The town was founded in 1853 by a group of prospectors and settlers who had come down from Oregon after hearing reports that there was a good harbor in the area. The bay did prove to be a good haven for ships, and soon the harbor was handling tons of supplies for settlers and miners farther inland and carrying off the gold, redwood lumber, and other produce of the region.

Like most of the other ports along this treacherous coast, however, Crescent City's harbor was not without danger for passing ships. Offshore rocks in the area claimed sailing vessels even before the city was founded, and within three years of the first settlers' arrival, a lighthouse was being built on a rocky point near the mouth of the harbor. It still stands today.

From the overlook, return the way you came.

Miles and Directions

0.0 Start at the signed trailhead opposite the Enderts Beach House garage.

0.1 Cross a 12-foot bridge. A few yards later, a spur trail heads right to Crescent Beach Picnic Area. Go straight.

1.3 Enderts Beach Road. Cross the road and continue along the trail on the other side.

1.4 Cross Cushing Creek via the 30-foot bridge and continue up the other side.

1.9 The trail pops out onto Enderts Beach Road. Turn right, heading uphill along the road.

2.0 The trail leaves the road, heading back into the brush on the right.

2.1 The trail reaches the overlook. This is the turnaround point; return the way you came.

4.2 Arrive back at the trailhead.

4 Hobbs Wall Trail and Trestle Loop

Highlights: A somewhat more adventurous hike around the thickly forested basin of Mill Creek's upper West Branch. The trail heads down through sparse old-growth fragments to the verdant creekside riparian zone surrounding Mill Creek Campground. From here a short stretch along the access road brings hikers to the wilder, more challenging ups and downs of the return loop.

Distance: 6.0-mile loop.

Approximate hiking time: 3 to 4 hours.

Best months: June through September.

Fees and permits: $2.00 day-use fee; $1.00 per person to hike or bike.

Maps: USGS map: Childs Hill, CA; *DeLorme: Northern California Atlas & Gazetteer:* Page 22 C3.

Special considerations: Check with the park beforehand to be sure summer seasonal bridges are in place.

Trail contact: Del Norte Coast Redwoods State Park, Crescent City; (707) 464-6101, ext. 5120; www.parks.ca.gov.

Finding the trailhead: From Crescent City, drive south 4 miles on U.S. Highway 101, then turn left (east) onto the Mill Creek Campground access road. (In winter the gate may be closed. If it is, park off the highway and walk down the campground access road to the trailhead.) Park alongside the road just inside the gate. The trail starts at the first bend in the road, on the right side, at a small trail sign marked HOBBS WALL TRAIL.

The Hike

The hike down into the emerald abyss of the West Branch Mill Creek drainage begins just inside the entrance gate to the Mill Creek Campground access road. An unassuming little trail sign marks the spot where the Hobbs Wall Trail crosses the road, just before the first curve in the road. Like

Hobbs Wall Trail and Trestle Loop

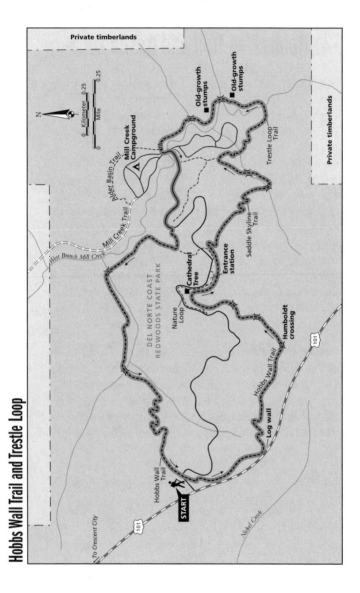

Private timberlands

Old-growth stumps

Old-growth stumps

Trestle Loop Trail

Private timberlands

Mill Creek Campground

Alder Basin Trail

Mill Creek Trail

West Branch Mill Creek

Saddle Skyline Trail

DEL NORTE COAST
REDWOODS STATE PARK

Cathedral Tree

Entrance station

Nature Loop

Humboldt crossing

Hobbs Wall Trail

Log wall

Hobbs Wall Trail

To Crescent City

START

Nickel Creek

101

101

N

0   0.25   Kilometer
0   0.25   Mile

the rest of the ridge, this part of the forest is dominated by old-growth redwoods. This hike circumnavigates the northeastern block of the park, from the ridge down to the creek and back up again near the park's northern boundary.

From the trailhead the hike first contours south along the ridge, soon arriving at a very peculiar structure. To the right of the trail, a massive wall is formed by the exposed ends of hundreds of redwood logs that have been stacked on top of one another and covered with gravel and dirt to form the foundation for US 101, above you on the right.

It is tempting to assume that the Hobbs Wall Trail gets its name from the wall of logs beneath US 101, but in fact the name comes from the nineteenth-century entrepreneurial firm Hobbs, Wall & Co., which had extensive land and timber holdings in Del Norte County from the mid-1800s to the 1940s. The company had a large mill and logging operation set up in the Mill Creek Valley just north of the park. Beginning in 1884 the company ran a short railway called the Crescent City & Smith River Railroad, which ran several miles up the Mill Creek drainage, well into the present park lands.

From the ridge the trail switchbacks down into the canyon, eventually arriving at the scene of this early railroad, on what is now called the Trestle Trail. Although there are a few remnants of the old train trestles, the most visible reminder of the lumber company's presence are the huge redwood stumps that fill the flats at the valley bottom.

After a short jaunt downstream, the Trestle Trail dumps hikers out into the extensive Mill Creek Campground, located on the flats around the creek. From here the trail heads left over the bridge and up the access road to a sharp bend. The trail then once again heads into the dense greenery of the forest, this time north of the access road. The final leg of the hike heads first down a steep series of stairs almost to the creek level, then back up in a wide loop to the ridge and trailhead.

Miles and Directions

0.0 Start at the small HOBBS WALL TRAIL sign on the south side of the entrance road, just inside the gate.

0.4 The ends of stacked logs form the foundation for the highway (to the right) and also form a wall alongside the trail.

0.9 The trail curves east, heading away from the highway and gently down into the valley.

1.2 Descend several steps and cross the creek via a long footbridge.

1.3 Hobbs Wall Trail ends at a T-junction. Nature Loop heads left to the entrance station and right to the Saddle Skyline Trail. Go right.

1.5 At the fork in the trail, veer right, heading uphill on the Saddle Skyline Trail.

2.1 Cross the creek via a 20-foot bridge.

2.3 At the junction, turn right onto the Trestle Loop.

2.7 The trail comes out onto a large, flat creekbed. Cross via the seasonal bridge, or wade if the water level allows during off-season. Continue straight into the forest on the other side.

3.25 The Alder Basin Trail heads up to the right. Continue straight.

3.3 Mill Creek Campground. At the paved road, turn left and cross the bridge. On the other side of the bridge, turn right and follow the park access road (the one with the EXIT sign) uphill.

3.8 The Saddle Skyline Trail crosses the road. Turn right onto the trail and head north into the forest.

4.0 At the junction, continue straight, heading back down into the valley.

5.8 The trail levels out at the burned-out old stump and heads south along the ridge.

6.0 Arrive back at the trailhead.

5 **Damnation Creek Trail**

Highlights: This hike follows a steep but very scenic trail, which offers the best of old-growth redwoods and rugged coastline. In spring the trail is sprinkled with a variety of wildflowers—most notably the distinctive three-leafed trillium, a showy native flower with white and pink blossoms. The trail ends at a beach next to a small, natural rock arch, carved by waves. Excellent tidepools can be explored at low tide.

Distance: 3.4 miles out and back.

Approximate hiking time: 2 hours.

Best months: April through October.

Fees and permits: No fees or permits required.

Maps: USGS maps: Childs Hill, CA, and Sister Rocks, CA; *DeLorme: Northern California Atlas & Gazetteer*: Page 22 C3.

Special considerations: At high tides, the beach at trail's end may be inaccessible.

Trail contact: Del Norte Redwoods State Park, Crescent City; (707) 464–6101, ext. 5064 or 5120.

Finding the trailhead: From Eureka, take U.S. Highway 101 north for 67 miles. North of the Klamath River the highway briefly skirts the ocean at Wilson Creek and False Klamath Cove before climbing steeply. As the highway veers inland away from the coast, it enters old-growth redwood forest. Park at the first turnout on the right, where the Coastal Trail crosses US 101. Start hiking where the Coastal Trail heads into the forest on the opposite (north) side of the road.

The Hike

The upper portion of this hike follows roughly in the footsteps of northwest California's patron pioneer, Jedediah

Damnation Creek Trail

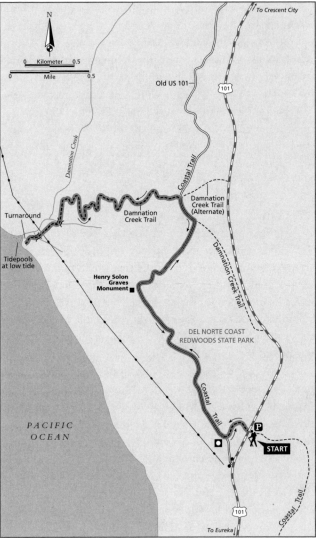

N

Kilometer 0 0.5
Mile 0 0.5

To Crescent City

Old US 101

101

Coastal Trail

Damnation Creek Trail (Alternate)

Damnation Creek

Damnation Creek Trail

Turnaround

Tidepools at low tide

Henry Solon Graves Monument

Damnation Creek Trail

DEL NORTE COAST REDWOODS STATE PARK

Coastal Trail

PACIFIC OCEAN

Coastal Trail

P

START

101

To Eureka

Coastal Trail

Smith—one of the most famous nineteenth-century mountain men. In 1827 the thirty-year-old Smith made his way up the Sacramento Valley, cutting west along the Trinity River to its confluence with the Klamath, and on downstream to the ocean. Smith and his party headed north from the mouth of the Klamath along the coast, reaching the Damnation Creek area in early June 1828. The difficulties of traveling with large pack animals in Redwood Country were daunting, to say the least. Once you see the jumbles of giant logs and dense vegetation that cover the forest floor here, you'll understand why. The journey was so difficult that the expedition sometimes managed to travel less than 2 miles a day!

The first part of the trail follows a piece of the Coastal Trail along a defunct section of the original US 101. If you scrape a few inches of duff off the trail, you'll find the pavement still mostly intact—right down to the yellow dividing line. The highway was diverted several years ago to avoid the coastline's slow but persistent slide into the ocean. Even today this phenomenon keeps the highway between Wilson Creek and the trailhead in constant need of repair.

From the old highway, the Damnation Creek Trail descends steeply through the dense forest that lines the deep Damnation Creek gully. The abundant fog creates an eerie, dramatic backdrop for the hike. As you make your way down through the tangled forest to the seemingly forgotten coastline, leather ferns perch high above the trail in the crooks of wind-twisted spruce and pine trees. The trail ends at a pristine, rocky cove, complete with stone arches and dramatic offshore rocks. At low tide these rocks reveal tidepools full of marine life. Mussels, sea urchins, anemones, and starfish can all be found clinging to the surf-pounded rocks. As wild-flowers come into bloom in spring, look for a splash of color in the tiny meadow above the beach.

Return the way you came.

Miles and Directions

0.0   Start at the junction of the Coastal Trail and US 101. The trail curves and heads west toward the coast.

0.1   The trail drops down onto an abandoned section of US 101. Turn right onto the old highway (now part of the Coastal Trail) and head north.

0.7   Damnation Creek Trail heads right (0.6 mile) to US 101. Continue straight on the Coastal Trail.

0.8   An alternate fork of Damnation Creek Trail heads right to US 101. The Coastal Trail continues north to Crescent City. Turn left onto Damnation Creek Trail and head downhill.

1.0   Halfway down to the beach, the trail begins a series of sharp switchbacks and descends rapidly.

1.7   Follow the faint path down to the right and down a series of wooden steps to the beach. The last few steps are rock. (Note: Be careful; they can be slippery.) This is the turn-around point. Return the way you came.

3.4   Arrive back at the trailhead.

6 Coastal Trail:
Yurok Loop to Hidden Beach

Highlights: A scenic hike along the Pacific coast through tunnels of wind-shaped cypress, alders, and dense coastal scrub, with plenty of spectacular views of this rugged and forbidding coastline. The turnaround point for the hike is tiny Hidden Beach, a quiet little cove accessible only by foot.

Distance: 2.0-mile reverse lollipop.

Approximate hiking time: 1 to 2 hours.

Best months: March through November.

Fees and permits: No fees or permits required.

Maps: USGS map: Requa, CA; *DeLorme: Northern California Atlas & Gazetteer*: Page 22 D2–3.

Trail contact: Redwood National and State Parks, Crescent City; (707) 464-6101; www.nps.gov/redw.

Finding the trailhead: From Crescent City, take U.S. Highway 101 south 14 miles to False Klamath Cove. At the south end of the cove, the highway leaves the coast and heads inland, passing a small picnic area to the south and west of the highway. Turn right into this picnic area (Lagoon Creek) and park. The Yurok Loop trailhead is at the west end of the parking lot.

The Hike

The hike begins at the Lagoon Creek Picnic Area, near where US 101 leaves the coast at False Klamath Cove and heads inland toward the town of Klamath, 5 miles to the south. The cove gets its name from the seafaring days, when sailors would frequently mistake it for the mouth of the Klamath. From the west end of the picnic area, the trail enters

Coastal Trail: Yurok Loop to Hidden Beach

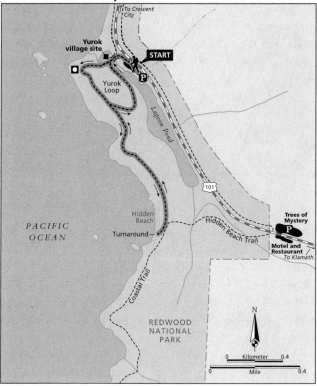

a clump of willows and turns left to cross a footbridge over the lagoon's outlet. Just on the other side of the bridge is where the Yurok Indian village of O'men once stood, but the spot is grown over now. A little farther on, the trail forks in a rather dramatic way, with both paths immediately plunging into brush so thick it forms tunnels over the trails. The hike follows the left fork up around the point to a fine overlook.

Offshore of the overlook, several sea stacks are visible, the largest of which is known to the Yurok as Olr'gr. It is said that there were once five brothers, the youngest of which was transformed into a supernatural being who made his home in that rock.

The trail continues around the point, following the coastline from the safety of the forest edge. This is part of the Coastal Trail, a network of trails that stretches up and down the ocean's edge more or less continuously from Oregon to Mexico. The local section of the trail also follows the route of an earlier Indian path, which connected the coastal villages and allowed for trade between settlements and neighboring tribes. About a mile south of the trailhead, the hike veers off to the right, following a steep, narrow path down to Hidden Beach. The small driftwood-strewn cove held little importance to the Yurok, since there were no fish-bearing streams emptying into it and no good village sites, but for today's hiker it is a sweet spot. Hidden Beach offers a quiet little hideaway, far from busy roads and tourist crowds, but within reach of an easy day hike.

From the beach the hike returns along the Coastal Trail to the southern end of the Yurok Loop. The return trail follows the inland portion of the loop, which passes through lush alder forests before dropping down to the lagoon's western edge and eventually returning to that first Y-junction near the trailhead.

Miles and Directions

0.0 Start at the Yurok Loop trailhead. Enter the forest on the broad path and turn left a few yards in, crossing the footbridge over the creek.

0.1 The trail forks, marking the start of the Yurok Loop. Take the right fork.

0.3 South end of the Yurok Loop Trail. The inland half of the loop heads left, but continue straight, to Hidden Beach. A few yards later, a spur cutoff comes in from the left, also leading to the Yurok Loop Trail. Go straight.

0.5 The trail pops out of the woods, revealing Hidden Beach ahead.

0.9 Just after you pass a large cypress, the Hidden Beach Trail heads left, leading to the Trees of Mystery complex. Continue straight. The spur to Hidden Beach soon heads down steeply to the right. Veer right onto the spur and follow it down.

1.0 Hidden Beach. This is the turnaround point. Enjoy the beach awhile, then return the way you came to the south end of the Yurok Loop.

1.7 Yurok Loop Junction. Turn right, following the inland half of the Yurok Loop Trail. A few yards later, a cutoff spur joins from the left. Continue straight.

1.8 The trail heads down a steep slope. The lagoon is visible to the right.

1.9 End of the Yurok Loop. Turn right and retrace the first part of the trail to the trailhead.

2.0 Arrive back at the trailhead.

7 Point St. George Trail

Highlights: A mellow stroll along bluffs overlooking a dramatic rocky coastline. An excellent hike for whale watching and eye-candy sunsets.

Distance: 2.2 miles out and back.

Approximate hiking time: 1 to 1.5 hours.

Best months: Good year-round.

Fees and permits: No fees or permits required.

Maps: USGS map: Crescent City, CA; *DeLorme: Northern California Atlas & Gazetteer*: Page 22 B1–2.

Trail contact: Tolowa Dunes State Park, Crescent City; (707) 464-6101, ext. 5112.

Finding the trailhead: From Crescent City, take U.S. Highway 101 north about 0.5 mile out of town. Exit onto Washington Boulevard and head west 3 miles until the road curves north, becoming Radio Road. Follow this another 1 mile until it dead-ends at a large gravel parking lot beside the former Coast Guard station.

The Hike

Tolowa Dunes State Park (formerly known as Lake Earle State Wildlife Area) is a roughly 5,000-acre preserve best known for its excellent wildlife habitat. The well-preserved wetlands here are an important stopover on the Pacific Flyway—a major migration route for bird species such as harlequin ducks, tundra swans, and Aleutian Canada geese. At the northern end of the park, the wild and scenic Smith River enters the pacific ocean, providing a transit route for another kind of migration as salmon and trout move upstream to spawn. But the park is worth visiting even if fish and fowl leave you cold. It encompasses a stretch of dramatic rocky coastline that is among the best in the state. Killer sunsets are

Point St. George Trail

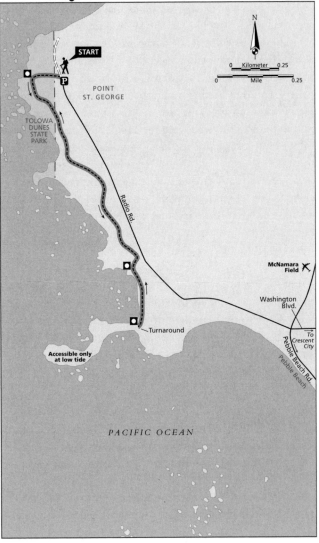

a regular occurrence, and the bluffs make an excellent platform for whale watching in late fall and midspring.

The hike begins in the large parking lot at the end of Radio Road. The lot is adjacent to a small group of buildings that once housed a Coast Guard station servicing local waters. The trail follows a faint path that skirts these buildings along the north side, heading in a more or less straight line to the bluffs overlooking the Pacific Ocean. At the edge of the bluffs, the trail then heads south along the precipice, meandering through grassy meadows as the fabulous panorama of the northern California coast sprawls off to the right. Every so often the path crosses or briefly joins an old roadbed, long since abandoned. There is no "real" trail here, but getting lost is not a problem—the treeless topography leaves little doubt as to your exact location.

The hike reaches its climax about a mile south of the trailhead, where low tides reveal a narrow gravel causeway that leads out to a massive knob of a sea stack. A gravel road leads down to the causeway from the bluffs. The base of the bluffs marks the turnaround point. After exploring the beach and causeway, return the way you came. Alternately, you can veer right a bit and return to the parking lot along the more direct (but less scenic) Radio Road.

Miles and Directions

0.0   Start in the northwest corner of the parking lot. Pass through the gate, and head left, following the faint foot path toward the bluffs, and keeping roughly parallel to the fence.

0.1   At the bluffs turn left, following the edge of the bluffs south along the coast.

0.7 The trail drops down onto a natural bench. The rocky beach and causeway are below to the right. Continue down toward them.

1.1 Turnaround point. Return the way you came, or follow Radio Road back to the trailhead.

2.2 Arrive back at the trailhead.

8 Carruthers Cove Trail

Highlights: An easy trail leading down through second-growth redwoods and coastal scrub to a secluded stretch of gorgeous beach.

Distance: 1.4 miles out and back.

Approximate hiking time: 1 to 1.5 hours.

Best months: April through October, but open year-round.

Fees and permits: No fees or permits required.

Maps: USGS map: Fern Canyon, CA; *DeLorme: Northern California Atlas & Gazetteer*: Page 32 A3.

Special considerations: If you plan to extend your hike down the coast, check tide charts beforehand; high tides can block the trail.

Trail contact: Prairie Creek Redwoods State Park, Orick; (707) 464-6101, ext. 5301.

Finding the trailhead: From Prairie Creek State Park headquarters, head north along Newton B. Drury Scenic Parkway about 8 miles, then turn left onto Coastal Drive. Head west on Coastal Drive 0.9 mile, and park in the gravel turnout on the left side of the road. The trail starts at the small trail sign.

The Hike

The trailhead for this hike is a small turnout on the Coastal Drive, a loop of bad road that follows the coast around from the northern end of Prairie Creek Redwoods State Park to the mouth of the Klamath River. This road was the original U.S. Highway 101, eventually abandoned in favor of an inland route due to its unfortunate tendency to slowly slide into the Pacific. Numerous dips and broken pavement mar the road, which is constantly in need of attention, even without major traffic. Luckily, hikers need

Carruthers Cove Trail

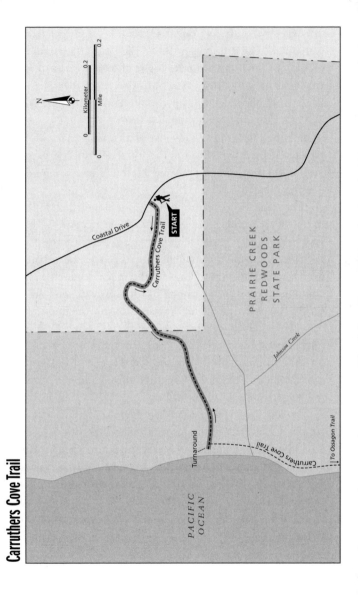

only travel a short section of Coastal Drive to get to the Carruthers Cove trailhead. From the small trail sign, the path drops down into a quiet forest of second-growth redwoods, scattered with spruce and a few other species. After a few yards, the singletrack path joins and follows the wide bed of a former logging road, now grown over and covered with duff. The gradual descent of the road makes for a pleasant stroll down through the forest, as sea breezes waft up through the trees, hinting at the stretch of coastline that is waiting below.

The trail contours around the gentle slopes, then follows the back of a ridge down as the grade becomes a little steeper. As it nears the beach, the trail becomes less steep and reverts to singletrack. Simultaneously, the vegetation changes from the second-growth forest of the upper slopes to a plant community dominated more by grasses and salt-tolerant shrubs and trees. With a last dramatic flourish, the forest gives way completely as the trail pops out onto the broad expanse of beach at Carruthers Cove. Off to the left, a large pond has formed at the mouth of Johnson Creek, right at the base of an old sea stack. Other sea stacks dot the coastline here, most still standing in the waves offshore.

For those who haven't satisfied their wanderlust yet, Carruthers Cove Trail continues south along the beach (use at low tide only), eventually connecting with the Ossagon Trail and emerging onto Newton B. Drury Scenic Parkway about 2 miles south. Otherwise, the beach is the turnaround point. If you plan to explore the beach, take note of where the trail exits the forest so that you can find it again when it's time to return.

Miles and Directions

0.0 Start at the small trail sign at the east end of the gravel turnout. The trail heads down into the forest.

0.6 The trail exits the forest onto the grassy upper beach. It is another 0.1 mile to the ocean. Take note of the spot so that you can find it when it's time to return.

1.4 Arrive back at the trailhead.

9 Ten Taypo–Hope Creek Loop

Highlights: This moderately strenuous hike explores rhododendron-laced old-growth redwood forest and some drier second growth in a pleasant 3.6-mile loop.

Distance: 3.6-mile loop.

Approximate hiking time: 2 to 3 hours.

Best months: April through October, but open year-round.

Fees and permits: No fees or permits required.

Maps: USGS map: Fern Canyon, CA; *DeLorme: Northern California Atlas & Gazetteer*: Page 32 A3.

Trail contact: Prairie Creek Redwoods State Park, Orick; (707) 464-6101, ext. 5301.

Finding the trailhead: From Eureka, head north 47 miles on U.S. Highway 101. Exit onto Newton B. Drury Scenic Parkway and continue another 7.4 miles to the Ten Taypo–Hope Creek Trail turnout at Mile Marker 132.74.

The Hike

Prairie Creek Redwoods State Park offers some of the easiest access to what are arguably the most impressive forests on the planet. The Ten Taypo–Hope Creek Loop is located at the northern end of all this green goodness, a little off the beaten path and therefore offering more of the seclusion that brings out the best in redwoods hikes. Standing alone in the misty, fern-filled understory, it is easy to feel yourself transported back to the age of dinosaurs, when redwoods first made their appearance on the world stage. This 3.6-mile loop traverses some old growth, mostly in the narrow Hope Creek drainage near the trailhead. From here the trail climbs

Ten Taypo-Hope Creek Loop

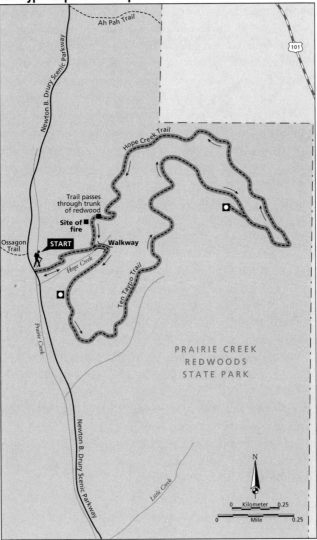

slowly but steadily to higher slopes that have seen logging activity within the past fifty to one hundred years.

At about halfway around the loop, the trail joins an old logging road for a portion of the hike that follows a low ridge. This section of the hike explores second-growth forests that are very different in mood and ecology from the lush old growth below. The forest is drier, ferns and other undergrowth are smaller and less prominent, and the forest floor is largely free of the jumbled rotting trunks of fallen giants. From the ridge, sounds of the nearby freeway can sometimes be heard off to the right.

After a short stint on the ridge, the trail leaves the old roadbed and begins a gradual descent. About halfway down, the trail becomes steeper and makes a few switchbacks before heading right through a burned-out redwood trunk. Although the damage to this tree was caused many years ago, a few turns later you will arrive at a much more recent burn. In June 2004 lightning struck a mature tree and started it slowly burning. The fire went unnoticed for two to three weeks until it had burned all the way down through the tree to the ground, where it began spreading. At that point, firefighters were called in, and they quickly contained the burn. All told, less than a quarter acre was damaged. One old-growth tree fell and others were charred, but luckily the damage was kept to a minimum.

Shortly beyond the fire zone, the trail rejoins the other end of the loop. Turn right here, and return along the first portion of the hike to the trailhead.

Miles and Directions

0.0   Start at the Ten Taypo-Hope Creek trailhead sign.

0.1   Junction. To the left is the Hope Creek Trail. Turn right onto the Ten Taypo Trail, heading down a few steps.

2.0   A spur trail heads back sharply to the right, leading down a few yards to a bench and overlook.

2.1   Junction. The trail turns left, following an old roadbed.

2.5   The trail leaves the roadbed and heads left into the forest.

3.3   The trail passes through the trunk of a redwood.

3.4   The trail heads through the site of a small fire.

3.5   End of the loop. Turn right and retrace the first portion of the hike to the trailhead.

3.6   Arrive back at the trailhead.

10 James Irvine–Miner's Ridge Loop

Highlights: An extended jaunt through one of the best remaining old-growth redwood forests. Beginning at the Prairie Creek Visitor Center, the trail follows burbling Godwood Creek through the prehistoric forest carpeted with lush ferns and skunk cabbage, then shows visitors a drier side of the redwoods as it climbs a ridge and returns via the Clintonia and Miner's Ridge Trails.

Distance: 6.2-mile loop.

Approximate hiking time: 2.5 to 3 hours.

Best months: April through October.

Fees and permits: $2.00 day-use fee.

Maps: USGS map: Fern Canyon, CA; *DeLorme: Northern California Atlas & Gazetteer*: Page 32 A3.

Trail contact: Prairie Creek Redwoods State Park, Orick; (707) 464-6101, ext. 5301; www.parks.ca.gov, www.nps.gov/redw.

Finding the trailhead: From Eureka, take U.S. Highway 101 north 47 miles and exit at Newton B. Drury Scenic Parkway. Turn left at the stop sign, pass under the highway, and head north another mile along the parkway to the Prairie Creek Redwoods State Park entrance, on the left. The trail starts at the large trail sign opposite the parking lot near the visitor center.

The Hike

The James Irvine Trail begins near the Prairie Creek Redwoods State Park Visitor Center and immediately delves into some of the most impressive old-growth redwood forest in California—or the world, for that matter. This and neighboring redwood parks are considered the crown jewels of California's state park system. Prairie Creek alone has 14,000

James Irvine–Miner's Ridge Loop

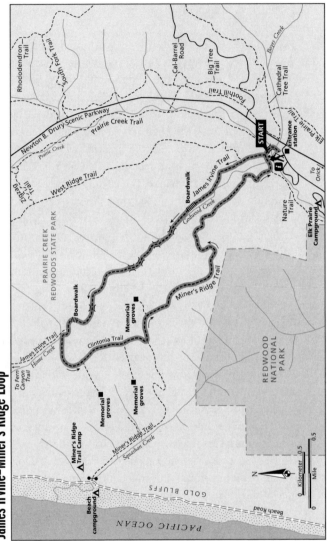

acres, much of it ancient forest, and an extensive network of trails to access it all.

The namesake prairie is at the heart of the park and seems a little out of place at first, given the huge accumulation of biomass in the surrounding forest. Long before the Europeans arrived, native Yurok people kept the prairie open by occasionally setting fire to the grass. This had the dual effect of pushing back the encroaching forest and encouraging tender new growth on the prairie, which in turn attracted large game such as deer and elk. The Yurok had a village nearby, close to where Davidson Road now joins Gold Bluffs Beach, and a trail led over the low ridge to the prairie. From here the path continued east, connecting the coastal village to the main Yurok population on the lower stretch of the Klamath River. Another trail followed roughly the same course as the modern James Irvine Trail, leading out to the coast and to villages farther north.

From the edge of the prairie near the visitor center, the trail heads north into the ancient redwood groves, immediately crossing a loop of Prairie Creek and heading upstream along a smaller tributary. This soggy bottomland adds a riparian element to the redwood environment, with big-leaf maple and the exotic-looking skunk cabbage fleshing out the normally sparse understory. The grade remains gentle for the first half of the hike as the trail follows the streambed up the increasingly narrow valley. At the head of the creek, the hike changes gears when you turn onto the steeper Clintonia Trail, climbing up to the much drier microclimate of Miner's Ridge. Here the hike heads inland again, along yet another historic route. This one is the Miner's Ridge Trail, remnant of a wagon road that once brought supplies and workers out to the gold mines at Fern Canyon and Gold

Bluffs Beach. The trail follows this southeast to the trailhead, along a straight redwood-lined ridge that puts the wooded avenues of Europe to shame.

Miles and Directions

0.0 Start at the visitor center trailhead (the large wooden sign next to a display case with elk antlers). Go down the wooden steps and across the bridge on James Irvine Trail.

0.05 Prairie Creek Trail heads right toward Zigzag Trail. Continue straight.

0.1 Nature Trail goes left toward Miner's Ridge Trail. Keep going straight on James Irvine Trail.

0.2 West Ridge Trail heads right. Continue straight.

2.8 The trail forks, with the right fork continuing to Fern Canyon. Take the left fork, following the Clintonia Trail up toward the junction with Miner's Ridge Trail.

3.8 Clintonia Trail dead-ends at Miner's Ridge Trail, which heads right (toward Gold Bluffs Beach) and left (toward the visitor center). Turn left onto Miner's Ridge Trail and follow it southeast along the ridge.

6.0 Miner's Ridge Trail ends at the junction with Nature Trail. Turn left onto Nature Trail and head toward the visitor center.

6.1 Turn right onto James Irvine Trail and retrace the first 0.1 mile to the trailhead.

6.2 Arrive back at the trailhead.

11 Fern Canyon Loop

Highlights: A short hike, made more challenging by the long, bumpy approach, but every bit worth the effort to find. The trail follows the bed of Home Creek up through a magical canyon, formed by hydraulic mining during the gold rush. Nature has outdone itself in healing these scars, with a lush carpet of ferns and moss hung like an emerald tapestry from the canyon's 40-foot walls. The return loop passes by the site of a gold-rush ghost town.

Distance: 1.0-mile loop.

Approximate hiking time: 1 hour.

Best months: April through October, but open year-round.

Fees and permits: $2.00 day-use fee.

Maps: USGS map: Fern Canyon, CA; *DeLorme: Northern California Atlas & Gazetteer*: Page 32 A3.

Special considerations: During the winter wet season, expect to get your feet wet.

Trail contact: Prairie Creek Redwoods State Park, Orick; (707) 464-6101, ext. 5301; www.parks.ca.gov, www.nps.gov/redw.

Finding the trailhead: From Eureka, head north 42 miles on U.S. Highway 101 to the town of Orick, then continue another 2 miles north before turning left onto Davidson Road. Follow this rough gravel road 4 miles to Gold Bluffs Beach and the entrance station (day-use fee collected); continue another 4 miles north to the end of the road at Fern Canyon trailhead.

The Hike

From the trailhead, the hike follows the streambed up through the canyon, where vegetation carpets the walls clear to the rim, far above. As you enter the mouth of Fern Canyon, you will no doubt notice the strange shape of the watershed, with its narrow, near-vertical walls and flat bottom. This shape is a

Fern Canyon Loop

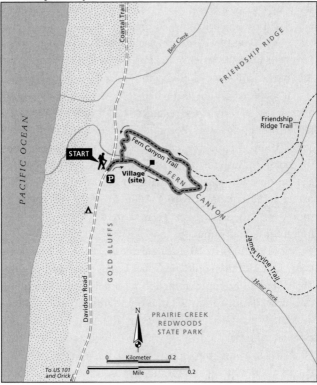

product of hydraulic mining, dating from the late 1800s. Hydraulic mining is a particularly destructive surface-mining method that involves washing away topsoil with high-pressure water cannons to uncover buried gold.

Although stripped of plant life by the mining activity, the years of inactivity have allowed the flora to recover nicely. The canyon is a gorgeous example of the lush flora that thrives in these temperate rain forests. Every square inch of the nearly vertical canyon walls are now covered with greenery, much of which belongs to one of several species of fern. Lady fern, wood fern, five-finger fern, deer fern, leather-leaf fern, and sword fern grow in the canyon and the surrounding forests, along with a host of mosses and other small plants.

In California, miners turned to hydraulic mining only after most of the "easy" nuggets had been recovered by placer mining (panning for gold). Miners searched for gold at the Bluffs on and off until the 1950s, but the area's mining industry was effectively dead by the turn of the twentieth century. The initial rush lasted from 1850 to 1852 and had a brief renaissance from 1866 to 1900. All told, the mines yielded only about $1 million worth of gold—not much for a gold mine.

Pioneer Edson Adams acquired the land around Fern Canyon soon after gold was discovered there in the early 1850s, and he promptly rented it out to a larger gold-mining operation. Before long a tiny community of half a dozen buildings had been established on the north rim of the canyon at Lincoln Prairie.

After reaching the upper end of the canyon, the trail climbs a series of steps to the rim and begins the return loop. The trail passes the "prairie"—actually just a small meadow—shortly before it reaches the mouth of the canyon, although nothing remains but ghosts and memories of the short-lived town that briefly thrived here.

Miles and Directions

0.0   Start at the kiosk on the north side of the parking lot. Follow the faint path across the gravel flats to the mouth of the canyon, and head upstream.

0.2 An old-growth trunk is down across the canyon. The trail passes under on the right.

0.5 Follow the steps up to the rim of Fern Canyon.

0.7 The James Irvine Trail heads right to the visitor center. Turn left and follow the Fern Canyon Trail west along the rim.

1.0 Descend steps to the mouth of Fern Canyon. Cross the gravel flats and return to the trailhead.

12 Trillium Falls Trail

Highlights: One of the newest trails in the park, Trillium Falls Trail was finished in 2002 and opens a whole new stretch of old-growth forest to exploration by eager hikers. Beginning at the Elk Meadows Day Use Area—recently restored from its longtime use as a lumber mill log deck—the trail also skirts the edges of the aptly named Elk Meadow, where dozens of Roosevelt elk can regularly be observed grazing on the soggy grass along meandering Prairie Creek.

Distance: 2.6-mile loop.
Approximate hiking time: 1.5 hours.
Best months: April through October, but open year-round.
Fees and permits: No fees or permits required.
Maps: USGS map: Orick, CA; *DeLorme: Northern California Atlas & Gazetteer*: Page 32 B3.
Trail contact: Redwood National and State Parks, Crescent City; (707) 464-6101; www.nps.gov/redw.

Finding the trailhead: From Eureka, take U.S. Highway 101 north 42 miles to Orick, then continue another 2 miles and turn left onto Davidson Road. Follow this for 0.4 mile, across Elk Meadow and over the bridge, then turn left into the Elk Meadow Day Use Area parking lot. The trailhead is at the sign near the restrooms.

The Hike

In the late 1850s hosts of eager men showed up to work the gold mines at the base of the nearby Gold Bluffs. One of those men, a young emigrant named Arthur Davidson, soon realized that a better living could be made in the dairy business. By 1890 Davidson was working his own ninety-acre dairy ranch centered around the present-day Elk Meadow Day Use Area. Four generations of the Davidson family continued to work

Trillium Falls Trail

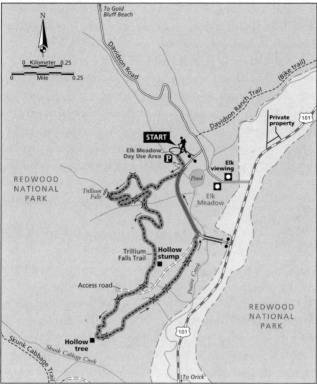

much of this land until 1991, when it was sold to Redwood National Park.

But the bucolic landscape you see today looked very different only a few years ago. Plans to build a railroad through the valley led to a right-of-way being split off the Davidson property in 1909. The railroad never happened, but the land changed hands several times. By World War II, it was owned by the Arcata Redwood Company. Eight acres of forest, meadow, and streambed were knocked flat and paved with asphalt to make a deck where huge redwood logs were stacked awaiting the buzz saws of Mill B. The mill was closed in 1970, and the log deck languished for a quarter century.

All that changed in 1996 when the national park acquired the mill site. Bulldozers went to work undoing the damage that bulldozers had originally caused. Between 1996 and 1999, crews restored the natural contours of the land, using buried tree stumps as a guide. The eight acres of asphalt were ripped up and used to create the base fill of the new day-use area. As a final touch, trail crews constructed the 2.6-mile-long Trillium Falls Trail through adjacent redwood groves.

The hike starts at the new day-use area parking lot, heading down a short asphalt path to the pond, already thick with recovering vegetation and a favorite with the local population of Roosevelt elk. From here the trail follows a gravel road a short distance south to the edge of the forest, where the singletrack Trillium Falls Trail heads up into the redwoods. Just less than half a mile up is the trail's namesake waterfall, a 10-foot cascade in a deep ravine, enlivened somewhat by the bright green foliage of a big-leaf maple.

From here the trail contours around the hill, leading hikers on a tour through classic redwood forests. Eventually the trail pops out on the gravel road and leads back to the creek. A side trail leads out across a long footbridge—an excellent vantage point for watching elk. The final leg follows the gravel road north along the edge of the wetlands to the trailhead.

Miles and Directions

0.0   Start at Davidson parking lot, Elk Meadow trailhead. Follow the asphalt path down toward the pond. Turn left at the first junction, then immediately right, following the path south along the pond.

0.1   About halfway past the pond, turn right onto the Trillium Falls Trail and follow the dirt path up into the forest.

0.5   Cross the creek on a long fiberglass/plastic bridge. To the right is Trillium Falls.

0.7   An old skid road crosses the trail. Continue straight.

1.0   Another old skid road heads up to the right. Continue straight.

1.3   The trail crosses a gravel road and continues on the other side. Go straight.

2.1   The trail dumps out onto a gravel road. Turn right on the road, heading downhill.

2.2   To the right, Davidson Trail heads over a long wooden bridge spanning Elk Meadow. Check out the bridge, then head north (straight) along the gravel road.

2.5   End of the loop. Continue straight, retracing the first leg of the trail to the parking lot.

2.6   Arrive back at the trailhead.

13 Ladybird Johnson Grove Trail

Highlights: This is a very short excursion through some very tall trees. Ladybird Johnson Grove was the location chosen for the dedication of Redwood National Park in 1969. The grove is named for former President Lyndon B. Johnson's wife, a woman known for her pioneering conservation work aimed at keeping America beautiful.

Distance: 1.5-mile loop.

Approximate hiking time: .5 to 1 hour.

Best months: April through October, but open year-round.

Fees and permits: No fees or permits required.

Maps: USGS map: Orick, CA; *DeLorme: Northern California Atlas & Gazetteer*: Page 32 B3.

Trail contact: Redwood National and State Parks, Crescent City; (707) 464-6101; www.nps.gov/redw.

Finding the trailhead: From Eureka, drive north on U.S. Highway 101 42 miles to Orick, then continue another 1.3 miles before turning right onto Bald Hills Road. Head up the hill (not suitable for large mobile homes or cars with weak brakes) for 2.5 miles, and turn right into the Ladybird Johnson Grove parking area. The trail starts at the kiosk at the west end of the parking lot.

The Hike

Although most hikes offer a pretty good workout for the hiker, the Ladybird Johnson Grove Trail gets most of its climbing done before you even get out of the car. From US 101, Bald Hills Road switchbacks up the ridge for 2.5 miles, gaining what seems like nearly that much in elevation before finally reaching the trailhead. The actual hike then begins with a flourish—crossing over the road via a gracefully arching wooden footbridge.

Ladybird Johnson Grove Trail

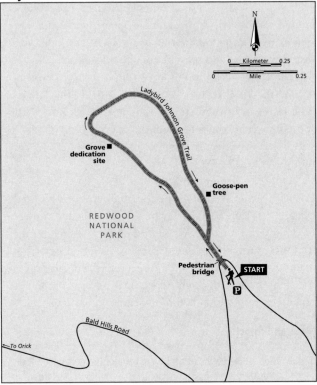

Once across the road, the trail quickly leaves the sound of struggling autos behind as it plunges deep into prime old-growth redwood groves. Since you are now on top of the ridge, there is little climbing to do. The trail has been "paved" with packed gravel, making the hike nearly wheelchair accessible. The gravel may seem like overkill to the hardened hiker, but it does more than just provide a smooth surface for visitors. The trees are visited by so many people each year that the constant trampling can compact the soil around the base of the giants, damaging their shallow root system and shortening their life spans. Gravel tread helps diffuse the pressure and prevent compacted soil.

The Ladybird Johnson Grove Trail describes a neat loop around the knoll at the western end of Bald Hills Ridge. A little less than halfway around the loop, the Ladybird Johnson Grove Trail comes to the little clearing—surrounded by stately redwood trunks—where the park dedication ceremony was held in 1969.

As well as inaugurating the new park, former President Richard Nixon dedicated the founding grove to his predecessor's first lady, Claudia Taylor Johnson—better known as Ladybird Johnson. Renowned for her work as one of America's most prominent conservationists, Ladybird was a good choice as a namesake for the grove. From the dedication site, the trail curves through old-growth giants around the remainder of the loop before returning to the trailhead.

Miles and Directions

0.0 Start at the trailhead at the west end of the parking lot. The hike starts by crossing the footbridge over Bald Hills Road.

0.2 The trail forks, beginning the loop. Take the left fork.

0.6 This clearing was the dedication site for the national park.

1.3 End of the loop. Turn left and return the way you came in.

1.5 Arrive back at the trailhead.

14 Tall Trees Grove Trail

Highlights: A short but impressive walk through the world's tallest trees. Besides redwoods, there are rhododendrons, giant ferns, and moss-hung maple trees, as well as access to wild Redwood Creek. The drive to preserve this grove led to the establishment of Redwood National Park. A permit is required to visit the Tall Trees Grove and is available free of charge from the visitor center just south of Orick.

Distance: 4.2-mile partial loop.

Approximate hiking time: 2 hours.

Best months: April through October, but open year-round.

Fees and permits: A free permit is required to access the trail.

Maps: USGS maps: Bald Hills, CA, and Rodgers Peak, CA; *DeLorme: Northern California Atlas & Gazetteer*: Page 33 C4.

Special considerations: Obtain a free permit at the Redwood National Park Visitor Center, just south of Orick on U.S. Highway 101. With the permit, you'll receive that day's gate combination.

Trail contact: Redwood National and State Parks, Crescent City; (707) 464–6101; www.nps.gov/redw.

Finding the trailhead: From Eureka, drive north 42 miles on US 101 to the town of Orick. Stop at the visitor center (open 9:00 A.M. to 5:00 P.M.) at the south end of town, and pick up a free permit. Just north of Orick, turn right onto Bald Hills Road and drive east 6.4 miles, then turn right onto the gravel Tall Trees Grove Access Road. Unlock the gate using the combination you were given with your permit; after closing the gate behind you, continue another 5.6 miles to the trailhead. The trail begins next to the small pavilion.

Tall Trees Grove Trail

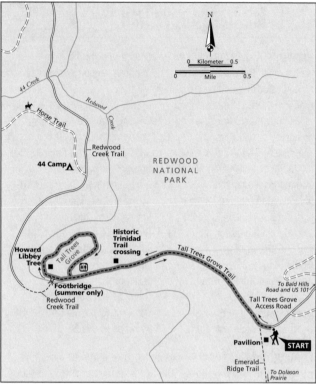

The Hike

Created in 1968, Redwood National Park is tiny as national parks go, and it is split into four isolated subsections, surrounded by state parks and private land. Nonetheless, it is still possible to find something approximating backcountry in the large southern end of the park, which encompasses the lower drainage of Redwood Creek.

The sheltered, fog-drenched location and nutrient-rich soil of the small floodplain provide ideal conditions for truly mammoth timber. Here on the edge of Redwood Creek stand some of the tallest trees on Earth. The official world-record holder—according to the National Park Service—stands a full 367.8 feet tall (more than 60 feet taller than the Statue of Liberty and its base combined). The second, third, and sixth tallest trees in the world are also in this grove.

Access to the grove is via a locked gate off of Bald Hills Road and a long, windy ex-logging road leading down through the young second growth of the upper slopes. At the end of the road is the trailhead for Tall Trees Grove and a small pavilion with a guest book for hikers. The first leg of the hike is a steep downhill, cool and shady beneath the dense canopy far above, with giant ferns and rhododendron thickets to both sides.

Eventually the trail reaches the floodplain and flattens out. This is where the giants are, well marked with signs along the loop. At several spots along the loop, it's possible to access the rocky bar alongside Redwood Creek, which is an excellent place to break out the food and have lunch. If you keep quiet, you have a good chance of spotting some of the abundant wildlife here. The second half of the lower loop winds through a grove of primal big-leaf maples. On sunny days, light passing through the maples' leaves dapples the forest floor in a bright green color that blends well with the thick moss carpeting the trees' limbs and trunks.

Upon completing the loop, return along the first leg of the hike to the trailhead.

Miles and Directions

0.0   Start next to the pavilion. Trail guides are located in a box at the trailhead, with descriptions corresponding to numbered posts along the path. Follow the trail as it heads downhill into the forest.

0.1   The Emerald Ridge Trail to Dolason Prairie heads left. Continue straight on Tall Trees Grove Trail.

1.5   The trail passes an outhouse on the right and enters Tall Trees Grove.

1.6   The trail forks, marking the start of the loop portion of the trail. Take the left fork. Shortly past the junction, Redwood Creek Trail heads left. Keep going straight.

1.7   (FYI: The official world's tallest tree is on the right.)

2.6   The loop ends back at the fork in the trail. Turn left and return the way you came.

4.2   Arrive back at the trailhead.

15 Dolason Prairie Trail

Highlights: The Dolason Prairie Trail is far from the tourist crowds that plague redwood groves along U.S. Highway 101. Beginning high in the Bald Hills, the trail explores prairies that local Native American populations once maintained with fire, then descends through thick forests to the old-growth redwood groves along Emerald Creek. Brooding fog often envelopes the valley, but on clear days the prairies offer excellent views.

Distance: 9.6 miles out and back.

Approximate hiking time: 4 to 5 hours.

Best months: April through October, but open year-round.

Fees and permits: No fees or permits required.

Maps: USGS maps: Rodgers Peak, CA, and Bald Hills, CA; *DeLorme: Northern California Atlas & Gazetteer*: Page 33 C4–5.

Trail contact: Redwood National and State Parks, Crescent City; (707) 464–6101; www.nps.gov/redw.

Finding the trailhead: From Orick, head north 1.3 miles on US 101, then turn right onto Bald Hills Road. Drive up the hill 9.5 miles to a fork in the road below a wildland fire station. Take the right (lower) fork, following the road another 1.3 miles to the Dolason Prairie trailhead parking lot, located in a clump of trees on the right. Turn right into the lot and park. The trailhead is located at the southeast corner of the parking lot, next to the kiosk.

The Hike

Sprawled across the ridgetop on the southwest side of Bald Hills Road, Dolason Prairie is part of a large patchwork of similar grasslands that dot the surrounding highlands. The prairies provide habitat for myriad plant and animal species. Thousand-pound Roosevelt elk bulls graze in the open space

Dolason Prairie Trail

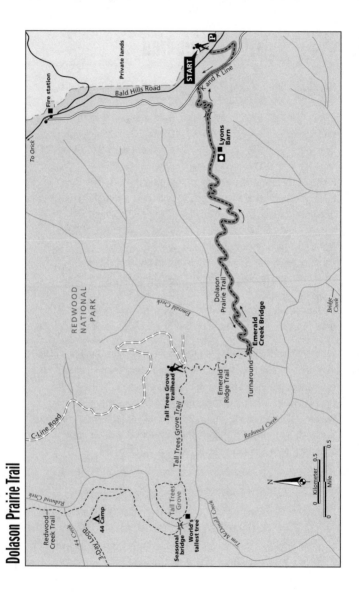

alongside brush rabbits and dusky-footed wood mice. Predators such as bobcats, coyotes, and the occasional mountain lion prowl the slopes, undeterred by the 5,000-odd insect species that also live here.

From the trailhead the hike follows a faint singletrack path down through the prairie, passing through a small clump of forest before emerging back out into the open on a gravel access road below. The road is closed to public automobile traffic but makes an excellent vantage point from which to survey the surrounding prairie. The open terrain also affords good vistas of the Redwood Creek drainage far below, provided the fog has not rolled in and obscured the view.

Following the road across the prairie, the trail veers off to the left just before the road reenters the forest, descending several switchbacks before popping out again onto prairie farther down. The historic Lyons Barn stands lonely and forgotten in the center of the meadow here. Built around 1914 by sheep-rancher Sherman Lyons, the barn served as a feeding station and shelter for his large flocks. This meadow, along with Dolason Prairie, belonged to the pioneering Lyons family from the 1860s until the 1960s, when it was sold to timber interests for logging. The Park Service acquired the land in 1978 as an expansion of the newly created Redwood National Park.

From the barn the trail descends rapidly, soon leaving the prairies behind and entering redwood forest. By the time the trail reaches the turnaround point at Emerald Creek Bridge, the second growth has merged into old growth, giving the steep-sloped watershed of Emerald Creek a primeval atmosphere. Giant trunks have fallen across the ravine, spanning the gap almost as well as the park's pedestrian bridge—an impressive 50-foot span perched equally high above the waterway.

Unless you want to extend your hike by continuing to Tall Trees Grove, return to the trailhead the way you came.

Miles and Directions

0.0 Start at the trailhead next to the kiosk in the southeast corner of the parking lot. The trail heads down to the left, toward a clump of trees.

0.1 The trail drops down onto an unused old road. Head right, following the trail.

0.2 The old roadbed curves left. Follow the footpath as it continues straight, out into open grass.

0.3 The trail drops down onto a gravel road. Turn right and continue on the road.

0.6 Just as the road is about to enter the forest, turn left onto a singletrack footpath, heading downhill.

1.1 Lyons Barn; continue across the meadow.

1.2 The trail enters brushy forest and begins a switchback descent.

2.1 A defunct trail heads back to the left. Turn right, continuing on the main trail.

2.9 On the left at a bend in the trail, an ancient redwood has tipped over, exposing an impressive root wad.

4.6 The trail passes a huge redwood with candelabra branches.

4.8 Emerald Creek Bridge, your turnaround point. Return the way you came. **Option:** Continue straight to the Tall Trees Trail. (FYI: Be very careful, the ramp on the east end is extremely slippery when moist.)

9.6 Arrive back at the trailhead.

16 Skunk Cabbage Trail

Highlights: This trail is a veritable cornucopia of habitats that leads through massive spruce and melancholy alder stands, into deep green canyons, and along pristine coastal bluffs. Along the way, hikers have a chance to see abundant wildflowers and the very plant that gives the trail its name, skunk cabbage. Very quiet, observant nature-watchers might even be lucky enough to catch a glimpse of elk through the trees.

Distance: 10.6 miles out and back.

Approximate hiking time: 5 to 6 hours.

Best months: April through October, but open year-round.

Fees and permits: No fees or permits required.

Maps: USGS map: Orick, CA; *DeLorme: Northern California Atlas & Gazetteer*: Page 32 B3.

Trail contact: Redwood National and State Parks, Crescent City; (707) 464-6101; www.nps.gov/redw.

Finding the trailhead: From Eureka, drive north 42 miles to the town of Orick. Just north of town, turn left at the sign for Skunk Cabbage Trail trailhead and continue another 0.6 mile to the trailhead. The trail begins where the road ends.

The Hike

The first section of the trail follows the path of an old logging road that cuts through a forest ravaged long ago. Nevertheless, there are still a number of remnant old-growth giants scattered throughout the area. Some of these redwoods were left as seed trees or were deemed unsuitable for the mill because they were twisted or hollow. Others were only broken stumps at the time the area was logged and

Skunk Cabbage Trail

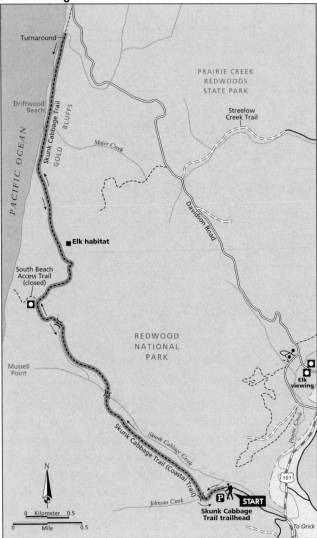

remain in nearly the same condition, thanks to redwood's natural rot resistance.

The second-growth forest that has replaced the ancient redwoods comprises mainly spruce and alder, trees that create a somber, isolated mood. The wetland along the floor of the drainage is filled with exotic-looking skunk cabbage, named for the strong odor of the leaf that surrounds its flower spike. A relative of the calla lily, the skunk cabbage blooms in spring and summer. A single burst of tiny blossoms is partially covered by a bright yellow hood, an arrangement that complements the plant's large, waxy leaves. The root and young leaf are edible after sufficient cooking and were used as a food source by some Native Americans and early miners.

After crossing the swamp, the trail heads up a fern-lined ravine and eventually reaches the crest of the coastal bluffs at the junction with the now-defunct South Beach Access Trail. The bluffs are steep and brushy here, so the trail ducks back inland to follow the ridge north through the forest. Game trails crisscross the ridges and hollows, and there are many open, flat spaces under the canopy where Roosevelt elk like to bed down. It's fairly unusual to see elk in the forest, but you have a chance of glimpsing one in this area. Keep a healthy distance from the elk, which are unpredictable.

The trail soon pops onto the bluffs again and quickly drops down to follow the beach northward. There are fields of driftwood on the beaches here, and some of the pieces are quite large. The hike ends at the creek crossing where Davidson Road leaves the woods and heads north along Gold Bluffs Beach. Return the way you came.

Miles and Directions

0.0   Start at the Skunk Cabbage Trail trailhead. Follow the Skunk Cabbage Trail (aka the Skunk Cabbage Section of the Coastal Trail) west into the forest.

0.5   (FYI: The swamp below to the right is full of the trail's namesake skunk cabbage.)

2.4   A spur trail used to lead down to the beach on the left, but it has been closed due to trail deterioration. There is a good view of the ocean from here. Continue to the right, following the main trail.

3.9   The trail exits the forest and switchbacks down the bluffs to the beach. At the bottom, turn right and head north along the narrow beach. There is no visible trail from here until the turnaround point.

4.4   The trail crosses a small creek. On the right is a large field of driftwood.

5.3   The trail reaches a wide creek. Davidson Road is visible as the trail exits the forest on the left and heads north along the dunes. This is the turnaround point for the hike. Return the way you came.

10.6   Arrive back at the trailhead.

17 **Rim Trail Loop**

Highlights: If you enjoy scenic vistas of rocky Pacific Ocean coastline, then this is the trail for you. The hike circumnavigates Patrick's Point State Park—a lesser known tourist attraction but a favorite with the locals. From the Rim Trail, numerous side trails lead to postcard-perfect views, which also offer excellent whale-watching opportunities. A bit of culture is thrown in for good measure, with the reconstructed traditional Yurok Indian village near the end of the hike.

Distance: 3.6-mile loop, with shorter variations possible.
Approximate hiking time: 2 to 3 hours.
Best months: April through October, but open year-round.
Fees and permits: $2.00 day-use fee.
Maps: USGS map: Trinidad, CA; *DeLorme: Northern California Atlas & Gazetteer*: Page 32 C2.
Trail contact: Patrick's Point State Park, 4150 Patrick's Point Drive, Trinidad; (707) 677-3570; www.parks.ca.gov.

Finding the trailhead: From Trinidad, head north on U.S. Highway 101 for 5 miles and take the second PATRICK'S POINT DRIVE exit. Turn left, passing under US 101 and following Patrick's Point Road around to the left. Turn right into the park entrance 0.5 mile later. Follow the park road past the entrance station and continue another 0.9 mile, following the signs for Agate Beach. Park at the Agate Beach parking lot. The trail begins at the south end of the lot, on the ocean side.

The Hike

The bulk of Patrick's Point State Park sits atop a raised marine terrace, perched about 200 feet above sea level. This position allows for breathtaking views from the many coastal overlooks scattered along the park's rocky cliffs. Beginning at the Agate Beach parking lot, the Rim Trail follows along the

Rim Trail Loop

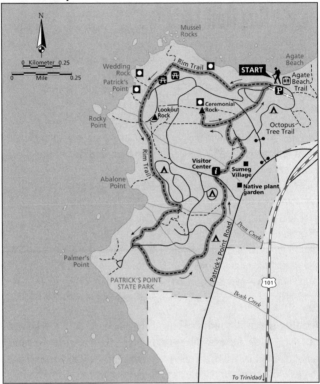

top of the marine terrace for much of the park's convoluted coastline. From it, several spur trails lead to rocky promontories that overlook the crashing waves below. Chief among these is Wedding Rock, a large knob jutting out into the Pacific, connected to the mainland only by a narrow wedge of land. Located about 0.75 mile from the trailhead, the rock can be reached via a 0.2-mile spur trail, which leads across the narrow land bridge and climbs a series of steps to reach the overlook. From here hikers can see the forbidding cliffs to their best advantage, and the thick fog that often rolls over the park only heightens the drama. Looking left down the coast from here will give you a view of the park's namesake, Patrick's Point.

The nearby promontory known as Lookout Rock was formed millions of years ago as wind and waves carved away the soft rock of the coastline. This area has been uplifted over the eons, raising the formation well out of reach of the waves that formed it. Another spur trail leads to the top of the small peak. The views are good from the summit, but only on fog-free days.

From Lookout Rock the trail circumnavigates the park on a scenic, if largely uneventful course. This changes when the trail passes the visitor center on the inland portion of the loop, arriving at Sumeg Village, a reconstructed traditional Yurok settlement. Far from being just an interpretive display for tourists, the village was constructed by surviving Yurok tribal members and is used by them for annual ceremonies. A nearby native plant garden is used by the tribe as a source of plant material for basket weaving and other traditional uses.

After exploring the village, the trail makes a short detour to Ceremonial Rock—another landlocked sea stack, similar to Lookout Rock—before heading back across a meadow and campground to the trailhead.

Miles and Directions

- **0.0** Start at the Rim Trail trailhead at the south end of the Agate Beach parking lot.
- **0.2** The trail forks, with the right fork leading a few yards to an overlook. Continue on the left fork, crossing a footbridge soon thereafter.

0.6 A picnic area is on the left, with a parking lot beyond. Take the right fork. Shortly thereafter you come to the junction with Wedding Rock. A spur trail heads right, down to the rock (0.2 mile). Continue straight.

0.7 A spur trail heads right to Patrick's Point (0.1 mile). (FYI: Patrick's Point, like Wedding Rock, is a great place to spot whales.) Go straight.

0.75 At the fork in the trail, the left branch heads up to the top of Lookout Rock (0.1 mile). Take the right branch.

0.8 At the junction, a spur trail to Rocky Point heads right (0.15 mile), while the Rim Trail continues to the left (straight). Go straight.

1.1 A spur trail goes left to Abalone Campground. Go straight. Several yards later the trail forks. To the right, a spur trail heads down to Abalone Point. Take the left fork.

1.5 At the junction, a spur heads left to the campground. Turn right, cross the footbridge, and turn right again on the other side, heading toward Palmer's Point.

1.6 The trail arrives at the other end of the Campfire Center Cut-off. Continue to the right on the Rim Trail, immediately crossing a small bridge.

1.9 The trail pops out onto the access road for Palmer's Point. Turn left, heading north on the road for several yards, then turn right again onto Rim Trail, where it reenters the woods on the other side of the road.

2.3 Beach Creek Group Camp. At the parking lot, head straight across the pavement and continue north on the other side, at the sign leading to Penn Creek.

2.4 At the junction, the trail to the left heads west to the Rim Trail; go right instead.

2.5 Cross the short section of causeway and head left on the other side, following the faint trail up along the stream. A few yards later, the trail crosses back over the drainage and becomes more obvious.

2.6 The trail takes a sharp left and crosses an 8-foot bridge.

2.7 At the four-way junction, head straight. A few yards later the trail reaches the entrance road near the entrance station. Cross the road and head toward the visitor center on the other side.

2.8 The trail continues in the upper right-hand corner of the visitor center parking lot. Just past the kiosk and the replica dugout canoe, the trail forks. Take the right fork to Sumeg Village. A few yards after that, a spur trail heads right to the native plant garden. Continue straight through Sumeg Village.

3.0 On the other side of the village is a picnic area, and after that a parking lot. At the parking lot, head left to the end of the lot, then left again to a second lot near the Red Alder Group Picnic Area.

3.1 At the midpoint of the second parking lot, turn left onto a connector trail leading into the woods. A few yards later, turn right at the junction. A few yards after that, turn left toward Ceremonial Rock.

3.2 At the T-junction turn left. Almost immediately, there is another T-junction. Turn left again, toward Ceremonial Rock.

3.3 A spur trail heads right up to the top of Ceremonial Rock (0.1 mile). This is the turnaround point. Head back to the last junction.

3.4 At the junction, head straight toward Agate Beach Campground.

3.5 The trail pops out into a meadow, then crosses the paved access road. Continue straight along the trail on the other side.

3.55 The trail arrives in Agate Campground. Head straight down the paved road. At the junction with the access road, turn right and follow the road back to the Agate Beach parking lot.

3.6 Arrive back at the trailhead.

18 Trinidad Head Loop

Highlights: This is a short but dramatic loop around Trinidad Head, a rocky promontory jutting out into the Pacific Ocean near the rustic fishing village of Trinidad. The hike offers either spectacular views of the ocean and a very scenic little fishing harbor or an eerie stroll through soupy fog, as the weather allows. Foghorns and lighthouses complete the scene.

Distance: 1.4-mile loop.

Approximate hiking time: 1 hour.

Best months: April through October, but open year-round.

Fees and permits: No fees or permits required.

Maps: USGS map: Trinidad, CA; *DeLorme: Northern California Atlas & Gazetteer*: Page 32 D2.

Trail contact: Trinidad Chamber of Commerce, Trinidad; (707) 677-1610.

Finding the trailhead: From U.S. Highway 101, exit at the main Trinidad exit and head into town on Main Street. About 0.2 mile into town, Main Street curves sharply left, becoming Stagecoach Road. Follow Stagecoach Road 0.1 mile to the end, then turn right onto Edwards Street. Continue another 0.3 mile down to the large gravel Sandy Beach parking lot. The trailhead is on the southeast corner of the parking lot, where steps head up the hill.

The Hike

The hike leads up a steep road, after having climbed a series of steps from the Sandy Beach parking lot. The road makes a switchback before long, and the hike continues around a more level singletrack path. Several benches are strung out along the western side of the loop, allowing hikers to stop and enjoy the view on fogless days.

Trinidad Head Loop

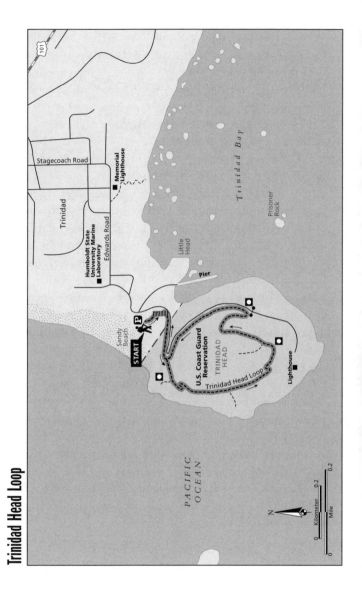

A lighthouse was built on the head in 1871, and the historic building is still used by the Coast Guard today, although it has been automated since 1974. When the trail reaches its southern apex, the lighthouse's squat tower can be seen far below to the right of the trail. To get a better idea of what it looks like close up, check out the duplicate lighthouse built by the town in 1948. It is located on the cliff along Edwards Road, right in town, and houses the lighthouse's original fourth-order Fresnel lens and fog bell.

Just above the viewing platform is a stone cross, set here by a local women's club in 1913 to mark the spot where Spanish explorers landed on Trinity Sunday back in 1775. The spot was named Trinidad for the holy day, and the land was formally claimed for Spain, although the local Yurok population already occupied a small village called Tsurai just below and to the east of the memorial lighthouse.

From the monument the trail heads up the grassy clearing to a gravel road, which leads down to the paved lighthouse access road. The access road is gated just above where the trail comes out, and a wide turnaround across the road offers some excellent views of the quaint little harbor. To the right, a large offshore rock can be seen guarding the entrance to the bay. Known as Prisoner Rock, it was once used as a handy spot to deposit rowdy drunks for the night. To the left is Trinidad's fishing pier, flanked by a smaller dome of rock known as Little Head.

From the overlook the trail follows the paved access road down past the loop junction to the wooden stairs, and from there to the trailhead.

Miles and Directions

0.0   Start at the bottom of the steps in the southeast corner of the parking lot. Climb the stairs, then head right on the paved road.

0.2   At the bend in the road, continue straight on the singletrack path. An overlook and a couple of benches are on the right, shortly after the junction.

0.7   The trail tops out at a clearing with a large stone cross monument. Below to the right is a small wooden platform, from which the old lighthouse and a wooden water tank can be seen far below. The trail turns left at the cross, heading uphill. When you reach the gravel road, turn right and head down the road.

0.9   The gravel road dead-ends onto a paved road. To the right is the gated entrance to the Coast Guard area. Straight ahead is a viewpoint overlooking Trinidad Bay. Turn left and head down the paved road.

1.2   The road meets the dirt path, which began the loop. Continue down the paved road to the stairs and trailhead.

1.4   Arrive back at the trailhead.

19 Arcata Community Forest Loop

Highlights: A leisurely jaunt through second-growth redwood forest along gravel and dirt tracks, just a stone's throw from the quirky college town of Arcata. Plenty of clearings and small meadows provide contrast to the deep shadows of the forest, and numerous connecting trails are available to customize the hike.

Distance: 4.0-mile lollipop.

Approximate hiking time: 1.5 to 2 hours.

Best months: April through October, but open year-round.

Fees and permits: No fees or permits required.

Maps: USGS maps: Arcata South, CA, and Arcata North, CA; *DeLorme: Northern California Atlas & Gazetteer*: Page 42 A–B3.

Special considerations: The Arcata Community Forest hosts volunteer workdays to do trail work, plant trees, and remove invasive species. Call for more information.

Trail contact: Department of Environmental Services, Arcata; (707) 822–8184; www.arcatacityhall.org.

Finding the trailhead: From downtown Arcata, take G Street north and turn right onto Fourteenth Street. Cross the bridge over U.S. Highway 101 and continue east on Fourteenth Street until it enters the Arcata Community Forest. When the road makes a sharp bend to the right, park at the gravel turnout on the side of the road. The trailhead is at the bulletin board on the east side of the road, just at the bend.

The Hike

Tucked up against the progressive little college town of Arcata is a jumble of densely forested hills that represent an ongoing experiment in modern silviculture. Dedicated in 1955, the Arcata Community Forest was originally acquired

Arcata Community Forest Loop

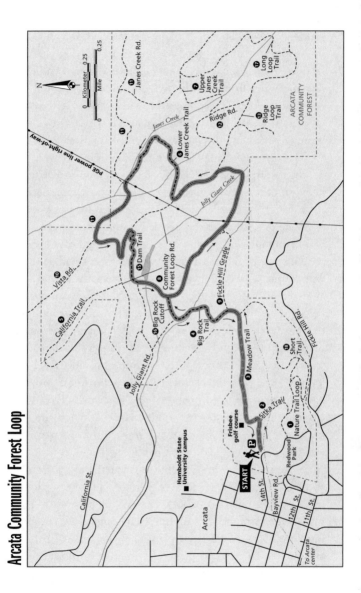

by the city as a source of drinking water, which was collected by building small reservoirs on the creeks flowing through the forest. This function became obsolete when Arcata began drawing water from the nearby Mad River in 1964, but the community forest has continued to serve the city as a source of education, wildlife habitat, sustainably harvested timber revenue, and numerous recreational opportunities.

The 600-plus acres of the community forest provide the main local attraction for local day hikers. Thanks to a 10-mile network of former logging roads and dirt paths, a variety of routes can be constructed. The route chosen for this book is only one of several possibilities, and it was chosen to create a good sampling of the forest in a medium-length day hike.

The trail begins at a turnout on the access road to Redwood Park, a large grassy park complete with playground and picnic tables, which provides the main interface between city dwellers and the forest. From the turnout, the trail heads steeply into the woods, quickly leaving the sounds of civilization behind and entering the lush realm of mature second-growth redwood forest. Because this area has been logged in the past, and occasionally still is, the forest does not have the pristine feel of national and state parks. Roads are closed to the public but are still used by staff. There are also signs of recent harvesting activity, in the form of fairly fresh log decks and forest debris left behind by logging.

Nevertheless, there is plenty of natural beauty around, and the visitor gets an idea of what an alternative to the usual "either thrash it or lock it away" dichotomy of land management might be. With the Arcata option, the community forest is managed equally for recreation, natural habitat, and timber. In order to make the first two possible, timber harvesting (last done in 2000) is done sustainably, according to the standards of the Forest Stewardship Council—and thus earns the eco-friendly SmartWood label. In addition, proceeds from the timber sales go into a forest trust fund, which is used to maintain the forest and to purchase additional forestland.

Miles and Directions

0.0 Start at the trailhead for the #3 Meadow Trail. Follow the dirt road steeply uphill.

0.1 The trail levels out at a small meadow and becomes dirt path. The #2 Sitka Trail heads straight; follow the #3 Meadow Trail as it switchbacks up to the left.

0.15 The trail tops out on a ridge and enters a small clearing. A Frisbee golf course is below and around you. Continue straight.

0.3 An unmarked trail heads down to the right. Continue on the #3 Meadow Trail as it curves to the right.

0.35 Another unmarked trail heads off to the left. Continue straight, passing through an open log deck/clearing.

0.4 An unmarked trail forks off to the left. Continue along the right fork.

0.5 At the gate, turn left onto the gravel road (#9 Fickle Hill Grade Trail) and continue to the first curve, then turn left again onto the dirt path (#4 Big Rock Trail).

0.65 At the short signpost turn right, following the #4 Big Rock Trail.

0.7 An unmarked trail heads right. Continue left as the trail switchbacks and heads down a few steps.

0.75 Turn right onto the #16 Big Rock Cutoff Trail, heading uphill.

0.85 The #16 Big Rock Cutoff Trail dead-ends onto a gravel road (#8 Community Forest Loop Road). Turn right onto #8 Community Forest Loop Road.

1.2 The trail tops out, and an unmarked trail heads left. Continue straight.

1.25 Take the left fork.

1.3 The #9 Fickle Hill Grade Trail heads downhill to the right; continue to the left on #8 Community Forest Loop Road. The trail then passes beneath a high-voltage power line.

1.65 You will see #12 Ridge Road heading off to the right. Continue straight on the #8 road.

1.75 Turn right onto the #6 Lower Janes Creek Trail (dirt path), heading down several steps.

2.0 The trail jogs left into the path of an old trail, crosses a sagging culvert, then jogs right again, heading up some steps.

2.35 At the clearing (under the power line again), turn left onto the gravel #11 Janes Creek Road.

2.55 You will see #10 Vista Road heading off to the right. Take the left fork, following #11 Janes Creek Road.

2.65 You will see #8 Community Forest Loop Road heading right. Continue to the left on the #11 road, heading uphill.

2.7 Turn right onto the #15 Dam Trail (dirt path), heading up a couple of steps to the ridge, then down the other side.

3.0 An old reservoir is on the left. At the junction, turn left onto the #8 road, crossing the earthwork dam.

3.1 Turn right onto the #16 Big Rock Cutoff Trail, retracing your route to the trailhead.

4.0 Arrive back at the trailhead.

20 Headwaters Forest Trail

Highlights: A decent hike up through second-growth forest to the fringe of one of northern California's newest and most politically charged parks: the Headwaters Preserve. The trail explores some history early on, passing by the site of Falk—once a flourishing logging boomtown, and now in the process of being rapidly reclaimed by the forest. Farther up, the path leads to the edge of an old-growth grove saved from clear-cutting by the efforts of environmental activists, public outcry, and political dealing. The preserve was created in the late 1990s, but some of the land may still be open to logging.

Distance: 11.2 miles out and back.

Approximate hiking time: 4 to 5 hours.

Best months: April through October, but open year-round.

Fees and permits: No fees or permits required.

Maps: USGS maps: McWhinney Creek, CA, and Fields Landing, CA; *DeLorme: Northern California Atlas & Gazetteer*: Page 42 C3.

Trail contact: Bureau of Land Management, Arcata; (707) 825-2300; www.ca.blm.gov/arcata/headwaters.html.

Finding the trailhead: From Eureka, take U.S. Highway 101 to the south end of Eureka, exit left (east) onto Herrick Road, then turn right onto Elk River Road. Follow Elk River Road south 1.7 miles to a fork in the road. Take the right fork (still Elk River Road) and continue another 3.4 miles to a bend in the road with a bridge on the right. Turn right, crossing over the bridge, and continue another 0.9 mile (still on Elk River Road) until the road dead-ends at the Headwaters Forest Reserve parking area. The trail starts at the bulletin board on the left.

Headwaters Forest Trail

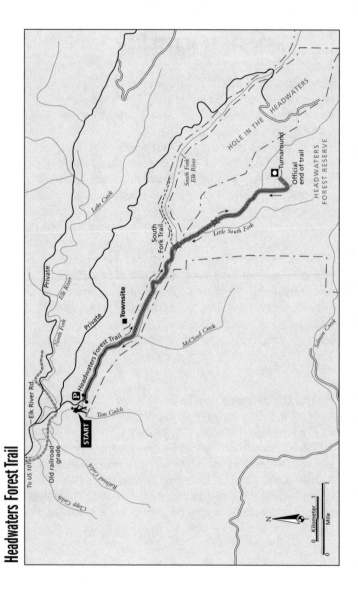

The Hike

The Headwaters Trail starts at the newly constructed trail-head and follows the old road—now closed to all but pedestrian traffic—for about a mile to the site of a former logging town called Falk. At its peak the town was home to around 400 people, including mill workers and their families, but the mill was closed in 1937. By 1979 Falk was a ghost town, and landowners burned and bulldozed the last remaining structures to avoid paying liability insurance. A leaflet can be picked up at the trailhead that explains more. A sign marks the meadow that was once the center of Falk. From here the trail continues southeast into the heart of the preserve.

The Headwaters Grove is a nearly 3,000-acre grove of old-growth redwoods located in the hills just east of Fortuna. The grove, which lies between isolated forests in Humboldt Redwoods State Park and Redwood National Park, is an important link for the gene pools of plants and animals in those two areas. The grove provides critical habitat for the endangered marbled murrelet and shelters headwaters that are home to the equally threatened coho salmon.

In the early 1980s, Headwaters Grove was the largest unprotected stand of old-growth redwoods in the world and belonged to the Pacific Lumber Company. In 1985 Charles Hurwitz's MAXXAM Corporation acquired the company in a hostile takeover and ramped up logging, soon threatening the headwaters. Environmentalists were horrified, and several attempts were made beginning in 1989 to purchase the groves for public parkland. A deal was finally sealed in 1999. State and federal governments purchased the Headwaters Grove and some smaller parcels for $380 million. Ironically, the final deal was opposed by many environmentalists because it left out several small groves of old-growth forest and left the so-called "Hole in the Headwaters" area—a 1,000-acre parcel of land within the Headwaters Forest Reserve that could still be logged by Pacific Lumber.

The trail leads past Falk into second-growth forest, climbing a series of steep slopes into the heart of the preserve and ending on the northern fringe of the Headwaters Grove. The turnaround point is a vista point—an old logging deck—that offers a view over Eureka to the northwest. Return the way you came.

Miles and Directions

0.0 Start at the bulletin board, and follow the paved Headwaters Trail east through an alder forest.

0.3 (FYI: The pair of yews on the right once flanked the entrance to someone's front yard. A cement paving stone can be seen between the yews.)

1.0 (FYI: The town of Falk once occupied the clearing to the left and the surrounding lands. The forest is encroaching rapidly on the townsite, and almost nothing remains of the buildings.)

3.0 South Fork Trail goes left along the narrow strip that hems in the Hole in the Headwaters. Continue to the right on the main trail, which changes from gravel to dirt.

5.0 The old bridge that used to span this creek has been removed. Follow the narrow footpath down to the right. Cross the creek and follow the footpath back up the other bank until it rejoins the road. Continue uphill on the road.

5.5 This is the official end of the trail. You can catch a glimpse of the old-growth Headwaters Grove straight ahead. Follow the road as it curves left to the vista point.

5.6 Reach the vista point. This is another old logging deck, next to a recovering clear-cut. Due to the lack of trees, to the left there is a good view of the ocean and the south end of Eureka. Straight ahead, on the other side of the ridge, is the Hole in the Headwaters. This spot is the turnaround point for the hike. Return the way you came.

11.2 Arrive back at the trailhead.

21 Hookton Slough Trail

Highlights: This short hike is an excursion into a landscape loved by wildlife but rarely visited by humans: the coastal wetland. Birders especially will find plenty to marvel at along this trail, which follows a historic dike out through the marsh along Hookton Slough, itself a branch of Humboldt Bay.

Distance: 3.0 miles out and back.

Approximate hiking time: 1.5 to 2 hours.

Best months: April through October, but open year-round.

Fees and permits: No fees or permits required.

Maps: USGS map: Fields Landing, CA; *DeLorme: Northern California Atlas & Gazetteer*: Page 42 C2.

Trail contact: Humboldt Bay National Wildlife Refuge, Loleta; (707) 733-5406; pacific.fws.gov/humboldtbay.

Finding the trailhead: From Eureka, take U.S. Highway 101 south 7 miles to the Hookton Road exit. Leave the highway, and at the stop sign continue straight on Hookton Road for another mile. Turn right onto the gravel Hookton Slough access road and follow it 0.1 mile to the parking area.

The Hike

More than 200 species of birds, including 4 endangered species, make their home in this refuge for at least part of the year. Migratory birds such as the black brant and marbled godwit are attracted to the extensive eelgrass beds and rich mudflats of Humboldt Bay, while raptors such as the peregrine falcon simply like to chase the other birds. The eelgrass habitat here is some of the best south of Alaska, making the bay a prime stopover along the Pacific Flyway migration route.

Hookton Slough Trail

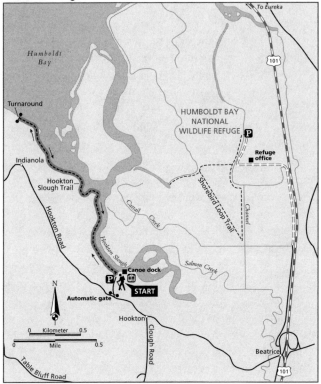

Humboldt Bay National Wildlife Refuge comprises multiple units scattered around the bay, totaling some 3,500 acres of protected habitat. The Salmon Creek and Hookton Slough units that together make up the southernmost portion of the refuge encompass more than 1,200 acres of wetland.

Prior to being included in the wildlife refuge system, the land was converted from the original salt marsh to agricultural land in the 1880s. Many of the dikes and ditches date from this period, as the marsh was drained and turned into grasslands for grazing cattle. When the feds took over, they set about restoring the land to create a variety of habitats. Mostly this meant working with the natural drainage patterns to create seasonally flooded marshes, permanent ponds, and tidal zones. Surprisingly, it also meant regularly mowing some areas in imitation of cattle grazing, since short-grass areas appeal to some species, including Aleutian geese. Today the refuge is home to many species of animals besides the birds, ranging from porcupine and mink to harbor seal and leopard shark. Take a closer look as you walk the Hookton Slough Trail, and you will probably see abundant signs of this diverse fauna.

From the trailhead the hike heads due west along the dike bordering Hookton Slough. The dike is topped by a gravel road used occasionally by refuge staff but closed to the public. As you work your way slowly out to the point, several interpretive signs appear periodically, going into greater depth about some of the natural cycles and wild residents of the refuge. The trail's turnaround point is a locked gate at the point where the dike rejoins dry land, near where Hookton Slough meets Humboldt Bay. Return the way you came to the trailhead.

Miles and Directions

- **0.0** Start at the kiosk on the west side of the parking lot. Head west along the dike.
- **0.7** The trail arrives at a point of land. The slough splits here, flowing around the large island ahead and to the left. Another interpretive sign marks the spot.

1.3 At the interpretive sign, the slough opens up into Humboldt Bay. The trail veers left.

1.5 The locked gate is the turnaround point. Return the way you came.

3.0 Arrive back at the trailhead.

22 Bull Creek Flats Loop

Highlights: This trail takes hikers on a classic stroll through the Rockefeller Forest, one of the largest tracts of contiguous uncut coastal redwoods in the world. The path wanders among the majestic trees, many of which are individually named for peculiar traits—such as the Flatiron Tree, known for its distinctive cross section. Beneath the canopy, plant lovers will find a variety of floral gems, including giant horsetail, iris, blue blossom, and sweet-scented bedstraw.

Distance: 9.2-mile loop.

Approximate hiking time: 4.5 hours.

Best months: April through October, but open year-round.

Fees and permits: No fees or permits required.

Maps: USGS maps: Weott, CA, and Bull Creek, CA; *DeLorme: Northern California Atlas & Gazetteer*: Page 52 B4.

Trail contact: Humboldt Redwoods State Park, Weott; (707) 946-2409; www.humboldtredwoods.org.

Finding the trailhead: From Eureka, head south 47 miles on U.S. Highway 101 to Humboldt Redwoods State Park. Exit at Mattole Road and turn right. Follow Mattole Road west 4.6 miles, and turn left at the sign for ROCKEFELLER FOREST: TALL TREE, FLATIRON TREE, AND GIANT TREE. Follow this road 200 feet to the parking area. The trail begins at the bulletin board.

The Hike

This trail showcases some of the park's most spectacular plant life. The path begins at the Big Tree parking area and immediately crosses the creek to visit some of the forest's so-called celebrity trees. These "famous" redwoods are well known for characteristics that make them special—even among the already unique trees. Among these stars are the

Bull Creek Flats Loop

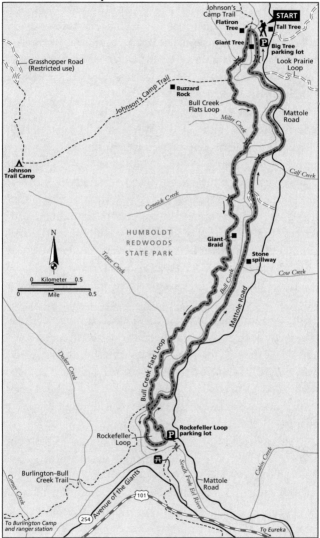

Johnson's Camp Trail

START
Tall Tree
Flatiron Tree

Giant Tree
Big Tree parking lot

Look Prairie Loop

Grasshopper Road (Restricted use)

Buzzard Rock

Johnson's Camp Trail

Bull Creek Flats Loop

Miller Creek

Mattole Road

Calf Creek

Johnson Trail Camp

Connick Creek

HUMBOLDT REDWOODS STATE PARK

Giant Braid

Stone spillway

Cow Creek

N

Bull Creek

Mattole Road

0   Kilometer   0.5
0   Mile   0.5

Tepee Creek

Decker Creek

Bull Creek Flats Loop

Rockefeller Loop parking lot

Rockefeller Loop

Burlington–Bull Creek Trail

Conner Creek

Cabin Creek

South Fork Eel River

Mattole Road

101

Avenue of the Giants

254

To Burlington Camp and ranger station

To Eureka

Flatiron Tree, so named for its unusual cross section, and the Giant Tree, noted for its size. The Giant Tree was not the tallest redwood on record, but it was considered by some to be the world's champion redwood by virtue of its combined height, circumference, and crown size. Unfortunately, both of these trees have recently fallen.

Leaving these celebrity redwoods behind, the trail heads east through the heart of the Rockefeller Forest. Officially termed a temperate rain forest, this park has been shown to possess more than seven times the biomass of tropical rain forests. Biomass is the recorded sum of all living and dead organic material in a given place. And there is an estimated 1,800 tons of it per acre in the old-growth stands of the park. From the dense mats of moss and ferns underfoot to the thick canopy suspended by the redwoods up to 350 feet overhead, almost everything you see here is—or was once—alive.

In the early part of the twentieth century, logging threatened to destroy the remaining ancient redwood groves. Some forward-thinking conservationists formed the Save-the-Redwoods League to combat the destruction. After taking a tour through the area, business tycoon J. D. Rockefeller was moved to donate $2 million to the league. The funds were used to purchase the 10,000 acres along Bull Creek, now named the Rockefeller Forest. It is through this forest that the Bull Creek Flats Loop wanders.

After crossing Bull Creek again, a side trail leads around the Rockefeller Loop before returning up the other side of the creek to the trailhead. This side of the stream has more second growth and several small glades laced with giant horsetail, sweet-scented bedstraw, and the ubiquitous redwood sorrel. Return the way you came, along the south bank of Bull Creek.

Miles and Directions

0.0 Start at the bulletin board in the Big Tree parking area. Cross Bull Creek, either via the temporary summer bridge or by wading in the off-season (at your own risk), and follow Bull Creek Flats Loop as it heads left along the creek.

0.05 A spur trail to the right leads a few yards to the Flatiron Tree. Continue straight on Bull Creek Flats Loop.

0.3 Johnson's Camp Trail heads uphill to the right. Continue straight, keeping parallel to Bull Creek.

1.9 (FYI: Keep an eye out for the Giant Braid, standing alongside the trail. This living curiosity consists of three redwood trunks that have grown twisted together.)

3.3 The trail skirts the base of an enormous log, making what seems like a U-turn. Follow it anyway, because it eventually doubles back again.

4.5 Burlington–Bull Creek Trail continues straight. Turn left and follow the Bull Creek Flats Loop down to the flat.

4.6 Cross Bull Creek again. Bull Creek Flats Loop heads left back up the other side of Bull Creek. Continue straight to explore the short Rockefeller Loop, which will return you to this junction shortly.

5.1 To the right is the parking lot for the Rockefeller Loop. Continue straight on the trail.

5.4 End of Rockefeller Loop. Turn right and return to the loop junction. At the junction, turn right and head upstream on Bull Creek Flats Loop.

8.2 The trail joins Mattole Road briefly. Continue straight on the road shoulder a few yards until the trail resumes, heading down to the left.

8.4 An unmarked trail veers off to the left. Continue along the right fork.

8.5 The trail joins Mattole Road again briefly. Continue straight along the road shoulder.

8.7 A picnic area has been set up in a turnout to the left of the road. Cross this open area and continue on Bull Creek Flats Loop as it enters the forest on the other side of the clearing. The trail enters the woods near the creek.

9.2 Arrive back at the Big Tree parking area and trailhead.

About the Author

Dan Brett is a certified wilderness fool, backcountry hiker, and freelance writer. His articles have appeared in *Backpacker, Country Back Roads,* and *California Blacksmith.* He is also the author of *Hike America: Northern California* (Globe Pequot) and *Hiking the Redwood Coast* (Falcon). He lives in Humboldt County with his wife, Mirjam.

Help Us Keep This Guide Up to Date

Every effort has been made by the author and editors to make this guide as accurate and useful as possible. However, many things can change after a guide is published—trails are rerouted, regulations change, facilities come under new management, etc.

We would love to hear from you concerning your experiences with this guide and how you feel it could be improved and kept up to date. While we may not be able to respond to all comments and suggestions, we'll take them to heart and we'll also make certain to share them with the author. Please send your comments and suggestions to the following address:

> The Globe Pequot Press
> Reader Response/Editorial Department
> P.O. Box 480
> Guilford, CT 06437

Or you may e-mail us at:

> editorial@GlobePequot.com

Thanks for your input, and happy travels!